Slavery's Ghost

*The Problem of Freedom
in the Age of Emancipation*

RICHARD FOLLETT
ERIC FONER
WALTER JOHNSON

The Johns Hopkins University Press
Baltimore

The Johns Hopkins University Press
2715 North Charles Street
Baltimore, Maryland 21218-4363
www.press.jhu.edu

Library of Congress Cataloging-in-Publication Data
Follett, Richard J., 1968–
Slavery's ghost : the problem of freedom in the age of emancipation /
Richard Follett, Eric Foner, Walter Johnson.
p. cm.
Includes bibliographical references and index.
ISBN-13: 978-1-4214-0235-2 (hardcover : alk. paper)
ISBN-10: 1-4214-0235-1 (hardcover : alk. paper)
ISBN-13: 978-1-4214-0236-9 (pbk. : alk. paper)
ISBN-10: 1-4214-0236-X (pbk. : alk. paper)
1. Slaves—Emancipation—United States. 2. Slavery—Social aspects—United States—
History. 3. Slavery—Psychological aspects—United States—History. 4. African Ameri-
cans—History—1863–1877. 5. Freedmen—United States—Social conditions.
6. African Americans—Race identity—History—19th century. 7. Slaveholders—Southern
States—History—19th century. 8. Plantation owners—United States—History—19th
century. 9. Identity (Psychology)—United States—History—19th century. I. Foner, Eric.
II. Johnson, Walter, 1967– III. Follett, Richard J., 1968– Legacies of enslavement.
IV. Foner, Eric. Abraham Lincoln, colonization, and the rights of Black America.
V. Johnson, Walter, 1967– Agency. VI. Title.
E453.F65 2011
306.3′620973—dc22   2011008169

A catalog record for this book is available from the British Library.

*Special discounts are available for bulk purchases of this book. For more information, please
contact Special Sales at 410-516-6936 or specialsales@press.jhu.edu.*

The Johns Hopkins University Press uses environmentally friendly book
materials, including recycled text paper that is composed of at least 30 percent
post-consumer waste, whenever possible.

CONTENTS

❧

FOREWORD

The Marcus Cunliffe Centre for the Study of the American South was founded in 2007 to facilitate cutting-edge research and dialogue on the history of the southern United States. Based at the University of Sussex in Brighton, England, the centre honors Marcus Cunliffe, professor of American Studies at the University of Sussex from 1965 to 1980. Professor Cunliffe authored more than a dozen books that ranged across the disciplines of history, literature, and politics and did much to create and advance the interdisciplinary approach to understanding America's attachments across the Atlantic. Whether he wrote of the institutional presidency or of George Washington's human and monumental record, of wage work and chattel slavery, of literary history or the history of property rights, Cunliffe's work always sought to bridge disciplinary boundaries and raise challenging questions about issues at the heart of the American experience that spoke to popular as well as academic audiences.

In the spirit of this tradition, the Marcus Cunliffe Centre hosts the annual Cunliffe Lecture Series, which brings together in the United Kingdom the very best scholars in the field to comment on critical issues in the southern past. These lectures are not intended to be exhaustive in scale or scope, but they do provide novel and incisive interpretations of contentious subjects. Like Professor Cunliffe's work, this lecture series (the first lectures of which are published here) aims to pose challenging questions and thus throw open fresh debates that will engage a broad audience of readers. To learn more and to follow the progress of the series, please visit our website: www.sussex.ac.uk/cunliffe.

Jarod Roll
Director
Marcus Cunliffe Centre
for the Study of the American South
University of Sussex

Introduction

✹

"FREEDOM"—THE RENOWNED ABOLITIONIST and fugitive slave Frederick Douglass wrote in 1855—is "the natural and inborn right of every member of the human family." Describing his life in chains, Douglass explained how the promise of freedom never entirely disappeared, despite the cruelest impositions of his southern masters. "I hated slavery, always, and the desire for freedom only needed a favorable breeze, to fan it into a blaze, at any moment. The thought of only being a creature of the *present* and the *past*, troubled me, and I longed to have a *future*—a future with hope in it." Douglass's stirring rhetoric provided mid-nineteenth-century Americans with a compelling narrative about the meaning of freedom and the consequences of its denial. Through autobiography and public speeches, Douglass insistently asked audiences to assess the concept and reality of freedom. And from the 1860s, as the nation descended into armed conflict, he urged his readership to consider both the promise and limits to citizenship for enslaved and emancipated African Americans alike. For Douglass, however, freedom encapsulated more than the abolition of slavery and political rights. To be free was to express one's self-respect, self-confidence, free will, and independence. Even a "slave in *form*" was a "freeman in *fact*" if that individual drew upon his or her self-reliance and the freedom of mind and body to resist the slave master culturally, spiritually, or physically. Military defeat in the Civil

War and the passage of the Thirteenth Amendment abolishing slavery brought the slaveholders to heel, but Douglass recognized that black freedom would not be easily attained. "Slavery," Douglass declared in December 1862, "has stamped its character too deeply and indelibly, to be blotted out in a day or a year, or even in a generation. The slave will yet remain in some sense a slave, long after the chains are taken from his limbs, and the master will retain much of the pride, the arrogance . . . and love of power, acquired by his former relation[s]."[1]

This book examines the concept of freedom and free will encapsulated in Douglass's words. It assesses the degree to which enslaved and freed people actively shaped their own worlds, and it considers the ideological, conceptual, and practical obstacles to freedom. In so doing, it considers two vital questions: first, the concept of "agency"—the degree to which black agricultural workers exercised free will and independence under slavery and emancipation or the extent to which a "slave in form," in Douglass's words, was a "freeman in fact." Second, the ways in which former bondspeople, slaveholders, and military and civic leaders (including President Abraham Lincoln) addressed both the abolition of slavery and the "problem of freedom." For the recently emancipated, the "problem" was to reconcile their economic and political liberties within the emerging free labor structure. As this book makes clear, however, ingrained patterns of behavior and racial thought combined with policy initiatives and economic circumstances to confine the range and latitude of black freedom in the age of emancipation. Collectively, the essays ask readers to consider how ideas about racial authority circulating in the mid-1800s shaped the material and conceptual limits to African American autonomy and indicate just how narrow and precarious the passageways out of slavery proved to be for enslaved workers in the rural South.

It was a poor inheritance from a revolution that had begun so promisingly during the Civil War. In singular contrast to the gradualist and compensated abolition programs of the Caribbean sugar islands, slave emancipation in the United States advanced by force of arms and by military defeat of the world's most powerful slaveholders. African Americans seized the opportunity afforded them as the institution of slavery eroded during the wartime years. Engaging in what scholars euphemistically call the "infrapolitics" of resistance under bondage, slaves exhibited their independence, humanity, and free will by shirking work, destroying property, running away, and willfully disobeying slaveholders. Equipped with the tools of racial and class resistance, enslaved African Americans flocked to Union lines when federal armies approached and, following the passage of Lincoln's Emancipation Proclamation, they engaged in what one of the earliest scholars of emancipation called a "general strike" and what one of the most recent scholars has named "the greatest slave rebellion in modern history." Both scholars were right. By downing tools, refusing to submit, and joining almost 180,000 African Americans who fought for the Union by war's end, enslaved peoples placed the issue of their own liberty and citizenship rights at the center of Union war aims and the postwar settlement. Formal emancipation in 1865 unleashed profound and revolutionary change. It freed a larger number of slaves than did the end of slavery in all other New World societies combined. Abolition, moreover, destroyed the legal principles of slavery, liquidated without compensation billions of dollars of private property held as human chattel, and forcibly replaced slavery with free labor.[2]

Emancipation, however, by no means assured long-term durable change for African Americans. As Frederick Douglass announced in May 1865, a month after Lincoln's assassination, "Slavery is not abolished until the black man has the ballot." Douglass had every reason to be pessimistic about the fate of his race. President Andrew Johnson's administration attempted to readmit the defeated southern states to the Union as swiftly as possible. Under Johnson's lenient policies, southern whites re-elected Confederate officeholders to power, introduced punitive black codes and vagrancy laws to restrict the movement and liberties of ex-slaves, and restored property to former slaveholders. For congressional Republicans who sought root-and-branch change and a wholesale reconstruction of southern society, Johnsonian Reconstruction seemed hollow and deceitful. As prominent Radical Thaddeus Stevens observed in 1865, "The whole fabric of southern society must be changed." Postwar Reconstruction must "revolutionize Southern institutions, habits, and manners . . . the foundation of their institutions must be broken up and re-laid," he insisted. Radical Republicans seized the political initiative in the November 1866 elections, and in March 1867 Congress passed the Reconstruction Act, thus beginning Radical or Congressional Reconstruction, which lasted until 1872–73.[3]

During this period, Congress extended civil and voting rights to former slaves, who seized the advantage wrought by such political change. They registered to vote for the party of Lincoln, they joined the Union Leagues, and they elected some two thousand African Americans to public office in the late 1860s and early 1870s. A small number of these held seats as federal congressmen and senators, but the real work of political and social reconstruction lay at the grassroots level, in small public offices, and in schoolhouses across the rural South where former slaves exercised the rights of citizenship and self-improvement. In the Fourteenth and Fifteenth Amendments, Congress placed the authority of the federal government behind an enlarged notion of citizenship but stopped short of redistributing land to former slaves. Without property of their own, rural black southerners returned to the land, much of which was still owned by former slaveholders, where they worked in a diverse array of labor systems, ranging from sharecropping in the cotton and tobacco regions to waged work in the sugar parishes of Louisiana. The degree to which ex-slaves leveraged their power and influence over politics and labor waned with the gradual retreat from Reconstruction in the mid-1870s. By 1877, southern whites (and the Democratic Party) had regained political control across the American South, aided in no small measure by white vigilante groups such as the Ku Klux Klan and White Leagues. These (so-called) Redeemer governments began to dismantle the civil and electoral rights accorded to African Americans during the height of Reconstruction.[4]

This brief account broadly conforms to the past twenty years of scholarship on emancipation and Reconstruction. The role African

Americans played in both the Civil War and Reconstruction receives considerable attention, and their struggle for freedom is placed as part of a broader continuum of black agency with its roots in slavery. Lincoln retains his magisterial presence over the nation as he guides the Union to victory with his moral compass fixed firmly (at least after 1862) on emancipation. But, as Frederick Douglass affirmed, black freedom was not easily attained, nor was it readily surrendered by white Americans. Dreading the day when the "white race has renewed its vows of patriotism and flowed back into its accustomed channels," Douglass had every reason to fear the "national deterioration" in race relations by the early 1870s. As Mississippian Horace Fulkerson observed, southern whites were "fixed in their determination to preserve their supremacy" whatever the cost.[5]

This book places the anger and despair of Douglass and Fulkerson in context by examining the ideological, experiential, and conceptual limits to African American freedom in the mid-nineteenth century. It does so on several interlocking levels, beginning with the concept of agency, before considering (at presidential and local levels) the multiple impediments to freedom and autonomous action faced by African Americans during the era of slavery and emancipation. Walter Johnson asks why historians of slavery have privileged the concept of agency— the degree to which enslaved peoples were able to construct their own world, remain independent of another's control, and exercise a degree of free will and self-ownership. As Johnson indicates, this scholarly legacy from the 1960s idealized the black slave as a "naturally autonomous, intrinsically self-determining, rights-bearing agent striving for 'freedom.'" Such theories continue to exercise considerable leverage among students of African American history. Indeed, so powerful has agency become as a means to understand black behavior under slavery and emancipation that one scholar recently called it "the captivity of a generation" of historians. As Johnson indicates, the ghost of slave agency haunts our interpretation of the past, but as he insists, this approach misjudges the extent to which "individual action" was embedded in the social condition of slavery. Urging readers to consider the limits and material determinants of agency, to develop a more nuanced understanding of historical power, and to better grasp the consciousness of those we study, while still insisting on the continuing importance of writing the history of slavery "from the bottom up," Johnson compels us to assess the degree to which the enslaved and recently emancipated were in fact subjects, not agents.[6]

The essays by Eric Foner and Richard Follett begin to answer Johnson's injunction. Both consider how ideas about racial authority endured as slavery gave way to free labor and citizenship in the 1860s and 1870s. As Foner indicates, Lincoln remained committed to the idea of repatriating black Americans outside the United States following slave emancipation. Even if he was implacably opposed to slavery, Lincoln—like many of his contemporaries—harbored considerable reservations about racial integration and black equality. Through the early years of the war, he favored a colonization scheme to physically separate the races or, at the very least, an apprenticeship system (such as that exercised in federally occupied Louisiana) to restrict African Americans to plantation labor.

If Lincoln's vision for freedpeople was ambivalent at best, the final essay underscores how southern slaveholding planters held tenaciously to their authority as land and labor lords in the years preceding and following emancipation. Focusing on the sugar-producing region of south Louisiana, Richard Follett indicates how racial concepts and plantation identities endured from slavery to freedom. Elite sugar planters, he argues, vigorously attempted to retain control of the plantation system and regimented black labor in the decades from the 1850s to the 1880s. African American slaves and freedpeople, by contrast, actively challenged planter authority. But, as Follett contends, the legacies of enslavement haunted the cane world. Drawing upon the power of federal, state, and personal authority, the sugar elite attempted to rein in what they considered to be the excesses of free labor and constrict African American freedom in the postwar years.

These essays are by no means exhaustive, although collectively they ask readers to assess the material and conceptual limits to African American freedom. They do not minimize or dispel the efforts made by slaves and freedpeople to exercise their collective and individual power in the workplace, in the quarters, and in the polling booth. Far from it. They do ask students and scholars, however, to reconsider the concept of agency and the degree to which racial and material factors confined black autonomy and freedom. Be it in Louisiana or elsewhere, material circumstances defined the degree to which slaves and freedpeople could shape their own lives. Structures of dominion that emerged and then persisted locally and nationally likewise proved singularly resilient. Frederick Douglass understood this fundamental reality. Writing in October 1870, he observed that "slavery has left its poison behind . . . both in the veins of the slaves and in those of the enslaver." The "settled habits of a nation," Douglass continued, are "mightier than statute." Douglass was right; the legacies and ideological inheritance of slavery have haunted Americans and the writing of their history from the nineteenth century to the present day.[7]

WALTER JOHNSON

Agency

❦

A Ghost Story

THIS IS THE STORY of a historian and a word. The historian is Herbert Gutman, generally recognized as the progenitor (for this is also a story of ancestors—ancestors recognized and disavowed—and even ghosts) of the "new labor history" in the United States. The word is *agency*. It was not Gutman's word, but it has come to haunt, to possess, his legacy. Put more directly: this is the story of how the injunction to write the history of enslaved people "from the bottom up" was compressed into the impulse to "give them back their agency." Running through historical writing about African Americans, the concept of "agency"—the capacity of individuals to act rationally and autonomously in pursuit of their own interests (almost always defined as the pursuit of civil rights and economic choice)—has emerged as the scarcely articulated master narrative, the common sense, of African American history. The point is not to question the importance of bottom-up histories but rather to suggest that students and scholars alike should refocus their attention on the material conditions and determinations of "agency": to think of historical actors as embedded rather than autonomous. As Karl Marx famously observed in 1852, "Men make their own history, but they do not make it just as they please; they do not make it under circumstances chosen by themselves, but under circumstances directly encountered, given and transmitted from the past."[1]

The story, at least as it is usually told, begins in the middle: 1964, to be precise, with the U.S. publication of E. P. Thompson's *The Making of the English Working Class*. In Thompson, Gutman found a model of how to write about the "agency" (Thompson's word) of working people, to which he would return for the rest of his life. Thompson framed his study as a response to an overly rigid and determinist version of Marxism. "The working class," Thompson wrote in describing the sort of determinism he was criticizing, "is assumed to have a real existence, which can be defined almost mathematically—so many men [*sic*—a masculinist universalism to which we will return] who stand in certain relation to the means of production. Once this is assumed it becomes possible to deduce the class-consciousness which 'it' ought to have (but seldom does have) if 'it' was properly aware of its own position and its real interests."[2]

In place of this strict ("almost mathematical") notion of economic base–ideological superstructure determination, Thompson proposed a notion of class as a "fluency," a dynamic process by which working people came to understand themselves as related to one another as they shaped radical and sometimes impossible notions of the future out of the confrontation between their present circumstances and their past lives: "Class happens when some men, as a result of common experiences (inherited or shared), feel and articulate the identity of their interests as between themselves, and as against other men whose interests are different from (and usually opposed to) theirs." And, furthermore, specifically addressing the question of the relationship of material life to ideology (the question of "determination") and of the translation of cultural history into class consciousness: "The class experience is largely determined by the productive relations into which men are born—or enter involuntarily. Class-consciousness is the way in which these experiences are handled in cultural terms: embodied in traditions, value-systems, ideas, and institutional forms."[3]

For Herbert Gutman, those came as welcome words. In 1963 Gutman had published "The Workers' Search for Power." The essay outlined a vision of labor history that focused on workers "themselves, their communities, and the day-to-day occurrences that shaped their outlook." Gutman later described the essay as a departure from older institutionally oriented labor history and "determinist and teleological" Marxism. Ten years later, Gutman published what quickly became the archetypical essay in "the new labor history": "Work, Culture, and Society in Industrializing America." The essay bore the imprint of "the cultural turn" in British Marxism; while reiterating his criticism of a labor history based on the history of unions to which "few" workers belonged, Gutman adopted a dynamic notion of working-class "culture as a resource." The essay recast traditional historical chronology in its comparative analysis of three moments in the history of the United States: the preindustrial (1815–1843), the industrial (1843–1893), and the mature industrial (1893–1919). Each era, Gutman argued, saw the introduction of first-generation proletarians to factories: in succession, rural American whites, urban artisans, and European immigrants became industrial wage workers. The history of labor in the United States, he concluded, had been decisively shaped by the repeated confrontation of "pre-industrial" or "pre-modern" workers and work habits with the demands of industrialization.[4]

Gutman's vision of the history of American labor was structured by a complex notion of historical time. "Work, Culture, and Society" urged the re-framing of U.S. history around the history of labor. In place of the orthodox framing of the history of the nineteenth-century United States as a more-or-less linear progression toward the Civil War, Gutman suggested a version of American history characterized by historical comparisons across time and space. The essay ranges freely through time and is characterized by suggestive and sometimes disorienting juxtapositions between time periods and groups of workers; a discussion of the wives and children of Nantucket whalers, for example, almost imperceptibly turns into a point about Jewish glove makers in Chicago in 1920.[5]

Gutman's overall argument is framed by a notion of historical repetition: at every turn, the history of labor in the United States had been characterized by resistance on the part of workers and violence on the part of owners. This history of repeated violence was itself structured by a notion of time: the idea that each confrontation was shaped by the sort of people workers were *before* they entered the factory, by the nested temporalities that linked the terms *first-generation* and *preindustrial*. Finally, there was the historian's own time. Toward the end of the essay, in a passage to which we will return, Gutman suggested that the process he was describing had "great implications for understanding the larger national American culture" of the 1960s and 1970s. As he did throughout his career, Gutman linked his history to his politics, drawing upon the past in his confrontation with the present much as he argued that American and immigrant workers had done throughout their history. By searching out forgotten possibilities and defeated hopes, he sought to reveal the contingency of the settled order and to model the possibility of its transformation.[6]

"Work, Culture, and Society" sought to generalize from its specific cases to a set of larger lessons about working-class history across time and place. Lowell mill girls with their "queer names" (Triphena, Plumy, Elgardy, etc.) and "outlandish fashions," journeymen tailors in the 1870s discussing "local and national politics, points of law, philosophy, physics, and religion," and Slavic steelworkers in Hammond, Indiana, kissing an ivory Christ as they "swore not to scab" in 1910 were, in effect, discrete in time and space but linked in their repetition of the same underlying process. In place of a Marxian notion of determination or historical process (the idea that the given organization of production at a time and place would shape or "determine" the ways in which workers understood their circumstances), Gutman was suggesting that American history had been structured by a set of meta-historical repetitions: culturally distinct though structurally analogous confrontations between past-rooted traditions and present conditions. Historians, Gutman wrote, should "focus on the particularities of both the groups involved and the society into which they enter. Transitions differ and depend upon the two at specific historical moments. But at all times there is a resultant tension." For Gutman, behind the ostensible historical specificity was an overarching (meta-historical) argument—a general theory according to which the specifics of time and place might be seen as the momentary hosts of a larger underlying process.[7]

At this point the story gets complicated. Actually, the story has been complicated for some time (although it is not always told that way), but at this point it turns into a ghost story. For the seemingly white labor history essay "Work, Culture, and Society" was haunted by more than a set of meta-historical repetitions. It was haunted by blackness: by what Toni Morrison has termed an "Africanist presence." Why refer to this as a haunting? Gutman was quite clear about the fact that "Work, Culture, and Society" was not an essay about black people. He said so in the text right at the start. Though they "deserved" a place in a comprehensive labor history, Gutman wrote, blacks would not be "given notice . . . the focus in these pages is on free white labor." And yet, rhetorically banished as they were to its margins, African Americans kept reappearing at crucial moments in Gutman's argument. Indeed, one might say that the entire essay is orchestrated by a blackness that is only occasionally—but always at crucial turns in the argument—visible in the text. Gutman's essay emerged at the juncture between the silencing of blackness that was its stated condition of possibility and the unspoken concern with African American history that animates its purpose.[8]

Peculiarly (unless one believes in ghosts), when Gutman collected his essays for republication in 1975, he introduced them with a joke about "the lives of Brother O'Neill, his wife, and their black friend." The joke was a fairly benign version of what once must have been a rougher-edged and more titillating joke (black-worker-meets-Irish-coworker's-wife was the premise; "he seemed just like anyone else" was the punchline) and had been told by the white woman activist Mary White Ovington to the Jamaican poet Claude McKay. For Ovington, and Gutman in turn, the story was emblematic of the "common interests" among workers once "caste lines disappear." That the "common interest" in question was the shared interest of male workers—white and black—in a single woman suggests the ways in which Gutman's resolution to the dilemmas of race was through the timeless verities of heterosex: a notion of interracial male subjectivity that brings blackness into a text from which it would almost as soon be rhetorically banished.[9]

Other images of the blackness that Gutman explicitly disavowed as the subject of his essay bolster the essay at several key junctures. Taken together, indeed, they might be said to serve as its unacknowledged architecture or, put differently, its animating spirit. The distinction between "culture" and "society" upon which the essay turns (and which Gutman used to replace the verticality of a base-superstructure notion of determination with a more horizontal and fluid account of working-class culture) has roots in a series of essays by the historical anthropologists Eric Wolf and Sidney Mintz about slavery and African American culture. Gutman included a long footnote that cited the writings of black leaders Frederick Douglass and W. E. B. Du Bois to argue that "the behavior and thought of rural and urban blacks fits the larger patterns suggested here in a special way" because "enslavement followed by racial exclusion sustained among blacks a culture that despite change remained preindustrial for more than merely two or three generations." He framed the conclusion to the essay with a quotation from the renowned black novelist Ralph Ellison: "Much of what gets into American literature gets there because so much is left out." "That also," Gutman noted, "has been the case in the writing of American working-class history." Indeed, expanding upon that point, one might argue that "Work, Culture, and Society" made sense, obtained coherence, at the juncture where what it said about African American history, the moments when it leaned on black history or black writers to steady its course through its argument about "free white labor," met what it left unsaid: the vexing unasked questions about black workers and black culture that haunt its edge.[10]

Perhaps the clearest of these meaning-making apparitions occurs when Gutman makes one of his characteristic efforts to link his historical analysis to contemporary political concerns by taking up the question of violence. Quoting from a *New York Times* symposium published in the aftermath of the nationwide series of black uprisings that followed the April 1968 assassination of Martin Luther King Jr.,

Gutman completed the historical circuit of his argument that "certain recurrent disorders and conflicts relate directly to the process that has continually 'adjusted' men and women to regular work habits and to the discipline of factory labor." The history of the white working class in the United States was thus recast as analytical prologue to that of black revolt in the 1960s. African Americans (disavowed as the subject of Gutman's essay) turned out to epitomize its contemporary relevance; "Work, Culture, and Society" turns out to be an essay that is finally configured around—preoccupied by—the very subject Gutman promised not to talk about.[11]

There are several ways to explain the revenant, or ghostly, blackness in Gutman's summary essay on the history of (white) work, culture, and society. Although he later attempted to shift attention from the broader context of the period in which he wrote to the more proximate intellectual influence of historians like E. P. Thompson (perhaps in accordance with his resistance to the idea of social determination), the years in which Gutman was writing "Work, Culture, and Society" were violent ones in the United States. In upstate New York, where Gutman was living, there were uprisings in Rochester in July 1964 and in Buffalo in June 1967 and again in April 1968. And so on: Hunter's Point in San Francisco in September 1966 (Gutman held a fellowship at the Center for Advanced Study in the Behavioral Science in Palo Alto during the academic year 1966–67); Attica in 1971. It is hard to believe that any sentient person, particularly as politically engaged a person as Herbert Gutman, could have been any less affected by these events than by reading Thompson's bottom-up history of "the poor stockinger, the Luddite cropper ... and the 'obsolete' hand-loom weaver" of the English past.[12]

And, in fact, in these years Gutman was doing a good deal of work on African American labor history. His essays on the history of black workers are pointedly anti-racist even as they stretch toward what was perhaps an unreachable aspiration: the discovery of a "usable past" of interracial-working-class solidarity and collective action in the industrializing United States. "The Negro and the United Mine Workers of America: The Career and Letters of Richard L. Davis and the United Mine Workers and Something of their Meaning, 1890–1900" is emblematic. The essay uses the letters of black miner, union organizer, and UMW National Executive Board member Richard L. Davis to trace the possibilities and limitations of interracial unionism at the turn of the century. Black unionists like Davis, it shows, were confronted with an extraordinary task. They faced, at once, the racism of white miners (which Gutman attributed mostly to the corporate-organized transportation of often-unwitting southern blacks to northern coal fields to serve as strikebreakers); the skepticism of African American workers, who associated unions with Democratic politics, race baiting, and white supremacy; and much of the leadership of the UMW and the American Federation of Labor (most notably the latter's leader, Samuel Gompers), who lustily, vituperatively, and repeatedly proved the skeptics right.[13]

Gutman's essay on the United Mine Workers (UMW) demonstrates a deep reading in the African American intellectual tradition; W. E. B. Du Bois, John Hope Franklin, and Pan-Africanist Rayford Logan take center stage, while European social historians E. P. Thompson and Eric Hobsbawm resort to the footnotes (three of them, to be precise). And it suggests the ferment, if not the distress, of a mind in transition. The title gradually shrinks its subject from "the Negro" to "the Career and Letters" of one "Negro," to "something of their meaning." The conclusion itself juxtaposes the aspirations and episodic successes of Davis and those like him to "the dominant influence" of the racist Gompers and the anti-unionist Booker T. Washington, suggesting—hoping?—the history of successful labor interracialism might be concealed in the still-to-be-studied recesses of local history. The essay provides less a historical legacy than a fleeting apparition: a vision of solidarity between working-class blacks and whites. It suggests that this vision—still treasured and yet so obviously, so impossibly, embattled in both the historical record and the world around him—was what was haunting Gutman's attempt to derive a general theory of (free-white) work, culture, and society in industrializing America.[14]

It might well be argued that what was actually haunting "Work, Culture, and Society" was not a ghost story where white is sometimes black, nor even the failures of interracial labor solidarity and the emergence of black power in the United States, but *The Black Family in Slavery and Freedom*, upon which Herbert Gutman had been working since at least 1968. *The Black Family* was Gutman's monumental effort to integrate the perplexities of race and slavery into the framework of "Work, Culture, and Society." The volume was cast as a response to what Gutman saw as a set of mischaracterizations of the history of African and African American slaves. In 1959, Stanley Elkins had published *Slavery: A Problem in American Institutional and Intellectual Life*, in which he argued that the cultural uprooting and familial separation represented by the Middle Passage were so great that they deprived African (and later African American) slaves of the cultural and communal resources necessary to resist slavery. "The new adjustment, to absolute power in a closed system, involved infantilization, and the detachment was so complete that little trace of prior (and thus alternative) cultural sanctions for behavior and personality remained for the descendents of the first generation," wrote Elkins. "Sambo," Elkins concluded, was a not a racist fantasy but a sociological necessity and historical reality: docile, infantile, pliable slaves had populated the whole of the history of slavery.[15]

Elkins's use of this most durable and harmful of caricatures might be explained (though not explained away) by his reading of black sociologist E. Franklin Frazier, his antiracist environmentalism, and his belief that analogizing slavery in the United States to the death camps of the Third Reich might aid in the elaboration of a Black-Jewish alliance in the struggle for civil rights. But it is hard to imagine that any would argue that Daniel Patrick Moynihan, assistant secretary of labor in the Kennedy administration, deserves the courtesy of a similar scholarly alibi. Moynihan's 1965 *The Negro Family: The Case for National Action* argued that whites who had been beguiled by "Negro protest" into believing that problems in the black community were due to poverty and discrimination were missing the point. The period of slavery, Moynihan argued, had been characterized by the indiscriminate separation of slave families and left in its wake (in the oft-repeated phrase) "a tangle of pathology" in the black community. Broken marriages, illegitimate births, female-headed households, unemployment, poverty, and welfare dependency all characterized a population that, it was ominously noted, was reproducing at a faster rate than were white people. Foremost among these problems was "matriarchy," or "the reversed roles of husband or wife," which produced social disorder, welfare dependency, and a burden of emasculating shame so great that black men might best be served by being inducted into the military, where they were proportionally under-represented.[16]

Gutman's *The Black Family* was framed as a direct response to the Moynihan report. The book used plantation account books, church records, travelers' accounts, the transcripts of Freedmen's Bureau inquests, and the narratives of former slaves recorded by the Works Progress Administration (WPA) in the 1930s to support a vindicationist account of black family life in slavery. The majority of slaves across the South, Gutman argued, lived in two-headed households; indeed, this supposedly normative pattern was quickly reestablished even in the era of the interstate slave trade, characterized as it was by an extraordinary level of family separation. Tracking patterns of marital exogamy (marrying outside given networks), Gutman argued that American slaves had an African-derived taboo on marriages of first cousins (a practice common among eighteenth- and nineteenth-century whites). Tracking naming patterns, he argued that slaves marked a historically deep notion of community (which in some cases stretched to the African past) through the names they gave their children (especially boys). Tracking the elaboration of "fictive kin" networks (again, an African pattern), he argued that family obligations were projected outward into a larger understanding of mutuality, generalized obligation, and community. *The Black Family* was what might be termed a dialectical negation, a mirror image, of the Moynihan report: it left in place *The Negro Family*'s patriarchal, hetero-normative, and family-centered notion of human flourishing and completion, even as it reversed the significance of these terms in relation to African American history.[17]

Finally, of course, there was Eugene D. Genovese. In *Roll, Jordan, Roll: The World the Slaves Made*, published in 1974, Genovese argued

that the closing of the Atlantic slave trade in 1808 materially transformed American slavery: an institution that had once relied on the
international trafficking of African slaves (a commercial modality of
social reproduction) was remade as a "domestic" institution—one
that depended upon the biological reproduction of the labor force to
ensure its survival. Concomitantly, as opposition to slavery grew both
in some regions of the South and outside it, slaveholding "reformers"
attempted to "humanize slavery" by "denouncing cruelty" and emphasizing the sense of obligation they felt to provide (food, clothing,
housing, entertainment—meanly measured and often subject to an
excise paid in extracted gratitude) for those whom they owned.[18]

For Genovese, this sort of "paternalism," determined within the
transformed material circumstances of southern slavery, was defined
by a set of reciprocities between master and slave that lurched from
familiarity and benevolence to cruelty and hatred. Paternalism, on
one level, obliged masters to consider their slaves as more than chattel property; this humanizing of slavery was vitally important for the
enslaved people who converted privileges doled out by the master
class into customary rights. Paternalism, however, cut both ways. The
obligations and reciprocities of the master-slave relationship linked
each individual to his or her owner. For Genovese, the personalization
of these links undermined solidarity among the slaves and defined
the limits of slave resistance. In contrast to the Caribbean or Brazil,
where mass slave revolts and flight (*marronage*) punctuated the history
of Atlantic slavery, he suggested that, in the United States, a dialectic
of accommodation and resistance defused collective action in favor of
small day-to-day acts of protest. While these daily acts diminished the
worst excesses of the exploitative system in which the enslaved lived,
they did not pose a revolutionary threat to the system as a whole. For
Genovese, paternalism expressed the class relationship and antagonism between masters and slaves in a way that allowed slaveholders
to convert their ownership into authority, to represent exploitation as
obligation, and to attain a fitful but nevertheless consequential "hegemony" over their slaves.

Genovese's notion of "hegemony" was derived from his reading of the Italian Marxist philosopher Antonio Gramsci. At certain moments in the history of class struggle, Gramsci argued, rule by a single class can be enforced not by violence but through general (if unwitting) assent to a limiting definition of the field of the politically possible. For Genovese, the ideology of "paternalism" provided such a definition of the institution of slavery: it described economic exploitation and class conflict in the idioms of family and community. In Genovese's formulation, much of what historians have come to term *resistance to slavery* did not weaken the authority of slaveholders but actually strengthened it. Malingering, shamming, stealing, and even more direct forms of violent resistance such as assault, arson, and murder, Genovese argued, localized and personalized what was actually a hemisphere-wide class conflict. They represented local adjustments along the fault line of class antagonism but not fully theorized and collectivized challenges to slavery-as-such. Day-to-day resistance to slavery was, by this argument, at best a "prepolitical" or even "apolitical" form of accommodation and at worst "pathetic nihilism."[19]

In 1976, Genovese and Elizabeth Fox-Genovese generalized the argument about class, culture, and politics made in *Roll, Jordan, Roll* into a broad critique of the practice of social history (including several snarky asides about Gutman's work on the black family in slavery). Social history, the Genoveses argued, had fallen away from the explicitly "socialist or at least anticapitalist political commitment" that had characterized the work of early practitioners and subsided into a "neoantiquarian swamp presided over by liberal ideologues." For the Genoveses, the proper subject of social history was the history of "classes contending for state power." The Genoveses were particularly pointed in their criticism of African and African American cultural history written outside a strict notion of material determination (in which the historical form of economic organization was taken to underlay and determine the parameters of politics and culture): "In emphasizing African origins, family life, and, in some measure, custom," the emergent emphasis on cultural history "denies the decisive importance of the master-slave dialectic—i.e., of the specific and historical ubiquitous form of class struggle—and no amount of 'radical' emphasis on black achievement and autonomy can disguise this retreat from a class interpretation to a politically anesthetized idealism." For the Genoveses, history was the history of class struggle ("the history of who rides whom and how"), and cultural history was simply a survey of the various mediating forms of that underlying (meta-historical) struggle.[20]

In *The Black Family* and several subsequent essays, Gutman expressed and then reiterated his commitment to a nondeterminist (and vindicationist) notion of African American culture, one that sharply diverged from the Genovese's notion of paternalistic hegemony and strict material determination. "Early-twentieth-century scholars nearly all believed that slaves could learn only from their owners so that slave culture . . . was at best 'imitative.' Later-twentieth-century historians and social scientists substitute behavioral 'models' for this crude belief but still often contend that slave belief and behavior involved little more than responses to master-sponsored external stimuli." Turning specifically to *Roll, Jordan, Roll*, Gutman argued that patterns of cultural affiliation (never fully specified but assumed to be indexed by naming patterns) among Africans and African Americans long antedated the emergence of the notion of slaveholding "paternalism," around which Genovese's book was framed. "Mid-nineteenth-century slaveowners—paternalists and nonpaternalists alike—therefore interacted with slaves who were the product of these earlier social and cultural developments." Where Genovese had accused culturalist social historians of allowing "the synchronic or spatial to predominate over the diachronic of narrative" (i.e., the struggle of contending classes for control of state power), Gutman responded that *Roll, Jordan, Roll* provided a "static" account of the interactions between masters and slaves, one that artificially separated enslaved people from their own history by superimposing upon it the history of their masters.[21]

The Black Family brought the terms through which Gutman understood African American history into conceptual alignment with those he had begun to work out in "Work, Culture, and Society." For Gutman, intergenerational and quasi-kin linkages were "slave passageways through time," vessels through which the resources of African culture were drawn through the history of slavery and into the twentieth century. "What filled these passageways," he wrote in an essay spelling out the book's conclusions, "requires careful study, but their presence is indisputable and therefore restores slaves to the mainstream of historical analysis." With *The Black Family*, Gutman resolved the contradiction that had stymied his earlier work on "the black worker." While the history of "the American working class" had been riven by racism, undercut by nationalism, and gainsaid by feminism, it existed in the transhistorical analogy between the histories of native and immigrant white workers and black slaves. Each group drew upon its own cultural history—"cumulative traditions," "rules for everyday living"—as the workers confronted inequality; each transmitted their cultures through their families; each drew the past into the present as a "resource" for resistance; each was characterized by a historical process in which the roots of mutuality and collective obligation predated the supposedly determinative structures of economic exploitation. Underlying American history was a set of sociological correspondences that translated seeming differences into similarities.[22]

Over time, the debate between Gutman and Genovese became a touchstone in almost any discussion of "history from the bottom up"—a touchstone that began to magnetize social history according to two scarcely explained conditions. Gutman and Genovese used a debate about African American culture to support a contrasting set of propositions about the relationship of class to culture more generally: Gutman arguing that the history of African American culture in the New World stretched backward in time before the antebellum period and thus provided resources from "outside" the system of slavery; Genovese that African American cultural forms "emerged from the mechanisms of equilibrium within continuing class war." Because both Gutman's humanism and the Genoveses' Marxism depended upon limited and totalizing formulations of the identities of the historical subjects they described, debates in the field were often characterized by a set of unarticulated presumptions about the race-and-sex neutrality of the working class. And because those debates were often understood as being between a version of history characterized by an emphasis on "agency" versus a version of history characterized by an emphasis on "hegemony," the question of "determination" (central to both the version of Marxism that Gutman was resisting and the one Genovese was advocating) began to fall out of view.[23]

Gutman formalized this analytical foreshortening in a 1980 essay on what he termed "The Sartre Question." Gutman began by quoting the French philosopher: "The essential," Jean-Paul Sartre observed, "is not what 'one' has done to man, but what man does with what 'one' has done to him." And he continued by reworking this philosophical principle as a lesson about American history: "Sartre's emphasis redefines the important questions we should ask in studying the history of dependent American social classes: slaves and poor free blacks, immigrant and native-born wage earners, male and female blue- and white-collar workers, and union and non-union members ... Studying the choices working men and women made and how their behavior affected important historical processes enlarges our understanding of 'the condition of being human.'"[24] As he sought to explain his vision of history—his legacy—in the years before his tragic death in 1985, Gutman repeatedly returned to this inclusive (and totalizing) formulation.[25]

Gutman's attempts to interpret American history from the bottom up and to alloy the working class through his General Theory culminated in the American Social History Project (ASHP), which he cofounded in 1981. The project, especially in the shape of its 1991 textbook, *Who Built America?*, extended Gutman's legacy and created a new national synthesis that privileged social and labor history. Special attention was given to the values and traditions of working peoples and the ways in which they "affected and were affected by the more familiar economic, social, cultural, and political processes that together make up the national experience."[26]

Without suggesting that every member of the American historical profession read Gutman's 1980 essay (or, still less, fully embraced the precepts that framed the ASHP), it might nevertheless be argued that Gutman's essay on Sartre crystallizes—emblematizes—the terms of translation through which "social history" was made visible to itself as a project in American universities in the 1970s and 1980s (even as the question of "determination" that had originally motivated Gutman's critique gradually faded from view). In these years, forms of insurgent knowledge—Marxism, Black Nationalism, and Feminism (and their various combinations)—were being (contentiously, awkwardly, and incompletely) institutionalized in American universities. Gutman's General Theory and its associated prescriptions—"history from the bottom-up" and, ultimately, "agency"—provided the means or terms of translation through which these various projects could be made comprehensible to the historical profession at large. These were the terms in which social history became the "cultural dominant" in the historical profession: terms that described history in a way that also prescribed the integration of women and minorities into the mainstream of the historical profession. Their fulfillment—even their partial fulfillment—was a historiographical and political achievement of lasting significance, a legacy of transformation that should be credited to Herbert Gutman as much as any other scholar.[27]

And yet these terms of alliance and ascendency were also terms of containment and cover-up. The cover-up I am describing was unintentional and incomplete. The point is not that historians stopped writing in those dissident traditions, for they obviously did not, but that the implications of what they were saying were circulated—glossed, reviewed, critiqued, credited—through an ideological medium, a commonsense, incapable of transmitting the most radical, least assimilable aspects of their message. There are moments when the mostly evanescent process I am describing can be captured in incubus. "In his argument with Stalinism and determinist Marxism," Herbert Gutman suggested in a 1983 restatement of his general theory, "Sartre put it very well. He said that the essential question for study—this is a paraphrase—is not what has been done to men and women but what men and women do with what is done to them. That is also a Thompsonian formulation. And this is precisely what the best black writers have been writing for the past fifty years. W. E. B. Du Bois argued for this approach when he wrote *Black Reconstruction*, and it is what C. L. R. James's historical writings are about."[28]

Here we see the intellectual and ideological limits of the General Theory made manifest: the translation and subordination of the historical specificity of the African American intellectual tradition, and of other forms of historical difference (here summoned and then evacuated of meaning with the substitution of "men and women" for Sartre's "man") and even the measured British Marxism of E. P. Thompson, into a single, anachronistic lineage. Let me be more specific. Black nationalism, black Marxism, and black feminism, the traditions of Martin Delany and Marcus Garvey, of W. E. B. Du Bois and C. L. R. James, of Angela Davis and Alice Walker have long, specific, and yet complexly intertwined histories. As Nell Irvin Painter has suggested in questioning the applicability of European social theory to African American history, these traditions have been rendered as oppositions in dominant social theory: "Negro" and "human being"; "African" and "American"; "class" and "race"; "intellectual" and "activist"; "black" and "woman." And they remain active and vital traditions of inquiry. Whether you begin with the work of social historians Sterling Stuckey, Lawrence Levine, Michael Angelo Gomez, or Nikhil Pal Singh on black nationalism; Sidney Mintz, Ira Berlin, Vincent Brown, or Stephanie Smallwood on diasporic materialism; Herbert Aptheker, Robin D. G. Kelley, David Roediger, Peter Linebaugh, Marcus Rediker, or Adam Green on black Marxism; Nell Irvin Painter, Darlene Clark Hine, Deborah Gray White, Tera Hunter, or Jennifer Morgan on black feminism, you are entering a discussion of—an argument about—the specificity of African and African American cultural forms and their historical transformation, the complex determinations of racialized identity and solidarity in relation to capitalist modernity, the gendered and sexualized character of racial alienation, subjectivity, and collectivity. They represent intellectual and political traditions evacuated of their specific meaning by the terms of Gutman's General Theory, their histories covered up by the misleadingly exclusive focus on the Thompsonian legacy of the New Social History.[29]

It must be said that the conversion of the dissident terms of radical historiography into the conventions of liberal humanism was perhaps a necessary condition of the integration of academic history departments during the Cold War. And it must be further said that Gutman's broadly liberal vision—one focused upon inclusion in the historical "mainstream" and the vindication of the "humanity" and "dignity" of the exploited and excluded—has a noble history and has done extraordinary work. Gutman's General Theory represented precisely the sort of "usable past" necessary to the progressive politics of the era in which he wrote: it framed American history as the prehistory of Civil Rights—racial integration and formal equality.

And yet, in more recent years, the General Theory's classically liberal and masculine notion of historical subjectivity—"one," "man"—and the elision or exclusion of the radical tradition in American historiography have come to haunt the profession in the guise of its most powerful word: *agency*. The space that in Gutman's early work had been filled by a sort of fill-in-the-blank deferral of historical, cultural, and sexual difference in favor of an emphasis on meta-historical similarity came in the General Theory to be filled with an underlying assumption of historical commonality, an assumption that reflected less an actual commonality than a selective reworking of various histories into a single strand. And, in our own time, in our own usage, that selective reworking has taken on the guise of a substantive account of historical subjectivity, an actually existing thing—the naturally autonomous, and intrinsically self-determining, and properly rights-bearing historical agent striving for "freedom." *Agency* has come to serve us not as a container by which disparate versions of historical subjectivity (the terms through which human beings understand themselves as historical actors) might be analyzed and compared to one another but as a crypto-liberal account of the thing itself.[30]

Ironically, perhaps uncannily, African American history generally and the history of slavery in particular have come to serve as the most abiding hosts of this corposant liberalism. In slavery studies, the "agency" discussion has usually worked along some variant of a circuit that ties "agency" (here defined as self-willed and autonomous action—what "one" does) to "humanity" (here defined as being a self-willed and autonomous actor) to "resistance" (here defined as preserving one's "humanity" by acting in a self-willed and autonomous fashion). Let me give you an example, which comes in the form of a sentence written by an eminent historian of slavery, though I freely admit I could at one time have written it myself: "Whenever and wherever masters, whether implicitly or explicitly, recognized the independent will and volition of their slaves, they acknowledged the humanity of their bondpeople. Extracting this admission was, in fact, a form of slave resistance, because slaves thereby opposed the dehumanization inherent in their status." Herein are agency, humanity, and resistance collapsed into one another and rendered up as a sort of parable of right-minded liberalism—the history of slavery is transformed into a parable about freedom. Alienated from the specificity of its own structural determinants and cultural idioms, African American history is here refashioned as the ultimate proving ground of what individuals—agents—can do in spite of their fetters.[31]

The idea of "the agent" as the essential subject of history has habited our history reading with an anachronistic (and generally unarticulated) assumption that beneath all history there lies a liberal individual subject waiting to be emancipated into the precise conditions that characterize the lives of the imperial bourgeoisie of the twenty-first century. Pushed to the side has been any genuine consideration of historical subjectivity. By formatting the question of human action as a simply binary opposition of (liberal) agency to (untheorized) power, the dominant discussion has begged—beggared, trampled, and ignored—the question of the material parameters—determinants—of historical subjectivity, the very questions that challenged and inspired Thompson (and Du Bois, and James, and Marx, and even, at least, the early Gutman). And not only that: even the questions of "standpoint" and "identity" that emerged out of cultural history to challenge the exclusions of historical orthodoxy (Marxist and otherwise) have been evacuated of much of their specific content (structurally determined or otherwise) in favor of this loosely liberal notion of the limits of historical and human possibility.[32]

"Agency" has transmogrified from a sort of analytical placeholder for various notions of (materially determined and culturally stipulated) historical action into a seemingly self-sufficient and exhaustive account of historical subjectivity. A question that was perhaps badly put in the beginning (structure vs. agency) but that nevertheless functioned as the occasion for a discussion of the question of "determination" and the past predicates of present action has been replaced with an even worse question. By framing our histories around the question of "autonomy" (here understood as a synonym for "agency" and even "humanity"), we have collapsed any consideration of the conditions of historical subjectivity and meaningful action into an adventitious and ahistorical binary (power vs. agency).

The "agent" as universal subject has thus been "deprived of real individual life and endowed with an unreal universality." The quotation is from Marx, who was criticizing a notion of political emancipation (citizenship) that did not attend to the social determinants of inequality. Under such conditions, he wrote, the real conditions of individual life—"distinctions of birth, social rank, education, occupation"—remained the salients of human existence even as they were replaced as official categories of governance by the notion of officially equal citizens. The "citizen," Marx wrote, was an "imaginary member of an illusory sovereignty," a governing abstraction whose power Marx went on to compare to that of the Holy Ghost. I am suggesting that there is a parallel (a homology, actually) between the vision of historiographical equality implied by Gutman's General Theory and formalized in the apotheosis of "agency" and the (merely) political emancipation analyzed by Marx. Each hypothesizes a serial and individual version of historical subjectivity—"one," "man," "agent," "citizen"—through which comparisons can be made and differences—actually existing, continuing historical and structural differences—disembodied.[33]

One way of revitalizing our understanding of the condition of enslaved humanity is through a renewed attention to the occasions of action: the material conditions of "agency." It has become fashion-able in recent years to oppose the term *work* to the term *culture*, or *power* to *agency*, and to use the former terms to bludgeon the latter, as if an increment added to the first set of terms forced an equal and opposite diminution of the latter on some sort of sliding scale. In a strange way, these arguments are mirror images of those they seem so concerned to oppose, those that they believe have overempha-sized the "degree" of enslaved "agency" and enslaved autonomy. But rather than trying to specify the terms of slaveholding "agency"— what sorts of action were available to enslaved people in what sorts of circumstances, what sorts of notions of commonality undergirded their solidarity—they have simply tried to cut it down to size. And yet, as any number of scholars (especially Raymond Williams, Stuart Hall, and William Sewell) have suggested, the question of "structural determination" need not be limited to the choice between a sort of turtles-all-the-way-down base-superstructure version of Marxism or a revisionist emphasis on "power" over "agency." Without accepting the untenable idea that the material conditions of human labor and reproduction directly determine the modes of understanding and expression—the ideology—through which people understand them-selves and confront their circumstances, one can nevertheless at-tempt to imagine slave agency in a world thick with its own histori-cal givenness. Rather than posing agency as the antidote to the indig-nities of exploitation (as Gutman would) or as a misleading panacea beloved of soft-minded progressives (as Genovese or countless other self-declared Real Marxists would have it), we might try to understand enslaved people's actions and ideas as, at once, fiercely determined— hedged in, limited, and shaped by the material conditions of their enslavement—and insistently transcendent—productive of new, cre-ative, vibrant, and sustaining forms of human being, commonality, and, ultimately, solidarity.

One might extend the emphasis on the material life (landscape, labor, reproduction, death) to a broader revaluation of culture and community in slavery, what I have elsewhere called "the condition of enslaved humanity." Slaves' love took the form of sharing food because they were starving; they succored the wounded because they had been beaten; they sheltered the escaped because they were being hunted; they talked about the departed because they had been sold away. These specific forms (and others like them) were hosts of the slaves' "agency," which was neither separable from the particular forms of their enslavement nor reducible to them. Those circumstances gave their actions material shape but did not exhaust their meaning or liquidate their force. Slaves acted in solidarity because they recognized their fellow slaves not as "agents" but as family members, lovers, Christians, Africans, blacks, workers, fellow travelers, women, men, and so forth. Even as their enslavement provided the specific occasion for their action, it occasioned the expression and ethics of care and practices of solidarity that transcended and actively reshaped their enslavement. Martin Delany, the prominent mid-nineteenth-century abolitionist and stalwart black nationalist, imagining the organization of a "general insurrection" of slaves in his 1861 novel *Blake*, described the dialectics of suffering and solidarity, the process by which the historical and material given-ness was worked into the lived experience of enslaved solidarity like this: "Such is the character of this organization, that punishment and misery are made the instruments of its propagation . . . Every blow you receive from the oppressor impresses the organization upon your mind." In Delany's formulation, the spirit of solidarity and resistance among slaves was a direct reflection of the given circumstances of their enslavement.[34]

In closing, let me be clear: in imagining the transubstantiation of "agency" into its material aspect, I am not questioning the importance of writing history "from the bottom up." Nor am I attempting to readjust the sliding switch away from "agency" and toward "power" or away from the oppressed and toward the oppressors along some abstract spectrum of historiographical favor. Nor, finally, am I suggesting that we should stop trying to think about the relationship between present and past in ethical terms. Quite the contrary. It is simply that I think that we can do better than "agency" (at least in its crypto-liberal guise) as a way of working toward the goals of a better, closer understanding of historical subjectivity, a more nuanced understanding of historical power, a more trenchant ethics of historical practice. Indeed, standing as we do at the juncture of seeming fulfillment of the promise of "civil rights" and the radical intensification of inequality—global inequality, racial inequality, class inequality, gender inequality, generational inequality, ecological inequality—standing at the juncture of the Age of Obama and the "global financial crisis," it is not simply that we can do better—we must. "Political emancipation," Marx wrote in a passage that reflects the terrific promises and incised limitations of both our history as it has been written and the history we are living, "is, of course, a big step forward. True, it is not the final form of human emancipation, but it is the final form of human emancipation within the hitherto existing world order. It goes without saying that we are speaking here of [something greater]: real, practical emancipation."[35]

ERIC FONER

Abraham Lincoln, Colonization, and the Rights of Black Americans

❧

IN APRIL 1876, Frederick Douglass delivered a celebrated oration at the unveiling of the Freedmen's Monument in Washington, D.C., a statue that depicted Abraham Lincoln conferring freedom on a kneeling slave. "No man," the former abolitionist remarked, "can say anything that is new of Abraham Lincoln." This has not, in the ensuing 130 years, deterred innumerable historians, biographers, journalists, lawyers, literary critics, and psychologists from trying to say something new about Lincoln. There are scores of biographies of every size, shape, and description, as well as books on Lincoln's views about everything from cigarette smoking to Judaism.[1]

In some ways, the past two decades have been a golden age of Lincoln scholarship. An unprecedented number of important works have appeared, both biographies and studies of one or another aspect of Lincoln's career, including his law practice, speeches, racial attitudes, and psychology. More still have been published during the bicentennial of his birth in 1809. In addition, thousands of primary sources directly relevant to Lincoln's life have for the first time become widely available to scholars in printed documentary collections, on compact disks, and in digitalized form on-line.

Many recent books offer striking new insights into Lincoln's career. Too often, however, the dramatic expansion of available material somehow seems to have gone hand in hand with a narrowing of focus.

Previous generations of scholars strove to place Lincoln in a broad political and social context. They published works with titles like *Lincoln and the Radicals*, *Lincoln and the Negro*, *Lincoln and the War Governors*. In too many recent studies, the wider world slips from view. To understand Lincoln, it seems, one has to study only the man himself.[2]

I have authored a book tracing the evolution of Lincoln's relationship with slavery and his ideas and policies about slavery and race in America. I admire Lincoln very much. Unlike much recent work, however, which takes Lincoln as the model of pragmatic politics and relegates other critics of slavery, especially the abolitionists, to the fringe as fanatics with no sense of practical politics, I want to situate Lincoln within the broad spectrum of antislavery opinion, ranging from immediate emancipation and the granting of full citizenship rights to blacks, to plans for gradual, compensated emancipation. Here, I want to focus on one neglected aspect of Lincoln's career—his long embrace of the idea of colonization; that is, settling the freed people outside the United States. This is by no means the whole of the story, but it does offer important insights into the evolution of Lincoln's thought on slavery, race, and American society.[3]

Lincoln, whose command of the English language surpassed that of nearly every other American president, did not produce a book during his lifetime (unless one counts the manuscript denying the divinity of the Bible that, according to local lore, he wrote in New Salem, Illinois, in the 1830s and then destroyed at the urging of friends). He did, however, put together two volumes of his speeches. One reproduced the Lincoln-Douglas debates. Less well known is his compilation of excerpts dealing with "negro equality." During the 1858 Senate campaign in Illinois, Democrats persistently represented Lincoln as an abolitionist who favored "the equality of the races, politically and socially." To fend off Democratic charges, Lincoln assembled a scrapbook of passages that, he wrote, "contain the substance of all I have ever said about 'negro equality.'" The volume remained in private hands until 1900, when a collector purchased it. It appeared in print three years later with the charming title, *Abraham Lincoln: His Book*.[4]

In a letter accompanying this book, Lincoln explained his stance on racial equality as of 1858. "I think the negro," he wrote, "is included in the word 'men' used in the Declaration of Independence" and that slavery was therefore wrong. But inalienable natural rights were one thing, and political and social rights were quite another. As Lincoln explained, "I have expressly disclaimed all intention to bring about social and political equality between the white and black races." This position distinguished Lincoln from the abolitionists, who advocated the incorporation of blacks as equal members of American society, and from Democrats like his rival Stephen A. Douglas, who insisted that the language of the Declaration applied only to whites. And what did Lincoln believe should become of black Americans when slavery ended? He included a passage from a speech that envisioned their return to Africa, which he called "their own native land," even though by this time nearly all of the slaves had been born in the United States.[5]

Lincoln's embrace of colonization—the government-promoted settlement of black Americans in Africa or some other location—was no passing fancy. He advocated the policy a number of times during the 1850s and pursued it avidly during the first two years of the Civil War. In his annual message to Congress of December 1862, Lincoln stated bluntly, "I cannot make it better known than it already is, that I strongly favor colonization." Gideon Welles, the wartime secretary of the navy, later chided "historians, biographers," and other commentators for making "slight, if any, allusion to it." This remains the case nearly a century and a half after Lincoln's death. True, for scholars like Lerone Bennett, who see Lincoln as an inveterate racist, colonization serves as exhibit number one. For Lincoln's far larger cadre of admirers, however, no aspect of his life has proved more puzzling. Most historians find it impossible to reconcile Lincoln's belief in colonization with his strong moral dislike of slavery. They either ignore his advocacy of the policy or fall back on the explanation that, as a consummate pragmatist, Lincoln could not have been serious about the idea of settling the African American population outside the country.[6]

A new look at Lincoln, slavery, and race must begin by taking colonization seriously as a political movement, an ideology, and a program that enjoyed remarkably broad support before and during the Civil War. Absurd as the plan may appear in retrospect, it seemed quite realistic to its advocates. Many large groups had been expelled from their homelands in modern times—for example, Spanish Muslims and Jews after 1492 and Acadians during the Seven Years War. Virtually the entire Indian population east of the Mississippi River had been removed by 1840. The mass migration of peoples was hardly unknown in the nineteenth century. In 1850, the prospect of colonizing the three million American slaves and free blacks seemed less unrealistic than did immediate abolition.

The idea of settling groups of New World blacks in Africa was a truly Atlantic idea, with advocates in the United States, the West Indies, Great Britain, and Africa itself. But as *Harper's Weekly* pointed out in 1862, nowhere else in the Western Hemisphere was it proposed "to extirpate the slaves after emancipation." Indeed, most post-emancipation societies desperately strove to keep the freed people from leaving the plantations. They never considered shipping the emancipated slaves elsewhere en masse. In this, as in other ways, the United States was exceptional.[7]

Colonization was hardly a fringe movement. Henry Clay and Thomas Jefferson, the statesmen most revered by Lincoln, favored colonization. So, at one time or another, did John Marshall, James Madison, Daniel Webster, and Andrew Jackson. Colonization allowed its advocates to imagine a society freed from both slavery and the unwanted presence of blacks. Taking the nineteenth century as a whole, colonization needs to be viewed in the context of other plans to determine the racial makeup of American society, including Indian removal and, later, Chinese exclusion. Advocates of colonization portrayed blacks, sometimes in the same breath, as depraved and dangerous outsiders, Christian imperialists, a class wronged by slavery, potential trading partners, and redeemers of Africa. The one constant was that they could not remain in America.

Thomas Jefferson prefaced his famous discussion of blacks' physical and intellectual capacities in *Notes on the State of Virginia* with an elaborate plan for gradual emancipation and colonization. Children born to slaves after a certain date would be educated at public expense, supplied with "arms, implements of household and of the handicraft arts, seeds, pairs of the useful domestic animals," and everything else necessary for them to thrive as a "free and independent people," and transported to Africa. Simultaneously, ships would be dispatched to other parts of the world to bring to the United States an "equal number of white inhabitants." Jefferson acknowledged that it seemed pointless to go to all this trouble to "replace one group of laborers with another." But, he warned, without colonization the end of slavery would be succeeded by racial warfare or, worse, racial "mixture." To his dying day, Jefferson remained committed to colonization. In 1824, he proposed that the federal government purchase and deport "the increase of each year" (that is, children), so that the slave population would age and eventually disappear. Jefferson acknowledged that some might object on humanitarian grounds to "the separation of infants from their mothers." But this, he insisted would be "straining at a gnat."[8]

The rapid growth of the free black population in the early republic spurred believers in a white America to action. Founded in 1816, the American Colonization Society (ACS) at first directed its efforts at removing blacks already free. Nonetheless, colonizationists frequently spoke of abolishing slavery gradually, peacefully, and without sectional conflict. Upper South planters and political leaders whose commitment to slavery appeared suspect dominated the ACS. None was more adamant in linking colonization with abolition than was Henry Clay.[9] Gradual emancipation coupled with colonization formed one part of Clay's American System, his plan for regional and national economic development that, he hoped, would reorient Kentucky into a modern, diversified economy modeled on the free-labor North. Slavery, he insisted, was why Kentucky lagged behind neighboring states in manufacturing and general prosperity. Clay succeeded James Madison as president of the ACS in 1836 and served until his own death sixteen years later. Lincoln's outlook on slavery closely paralleled that of Clay, who he called "my beau ideal of a statesman."[9]

Some African Americans shared the perspective of the colonization movement. Almost every printed report of the ACS included testimonials from blacks who had either gone to Africa or were anxious to do so. Throughout the nineteenth century, however, most black Americans rejected both voluntary emigration and government-sponsored efforts to encourage or coerce the entire black population to leave the country. Indeed, black hostility to colonization was one of the key catalysts for the rise of immediate abolitionism in the late 1820s and 1830s. The difference between colonization and abolitionism lay not only in their approach to getting rid of slavery but also in their view as to whether blacks could hope to achieve equal citizenship in this country.

The militant abolitionism that emerged in the 1830s, committed to making the United States a biracial nation, arose as the joining of two impulses—black anticolonization and white evangelicism and perfectionism. Through the attack on colonization, the modern idea of equality as something that knows no racial boundaries was born. Free blacks denied that racism was immutable and that a nation must be racially homogeneous. The black response to colonization powerfully affected white abolitionists. In his influential pamphlet, *Thoughts on African Colonization*, William Lloyd Garrison explained that his experience with vibrant free black communities inspired his conversion from colonization to abolition and racial equality.[10]

The assault by Garrison and others opened a chasm between militant abolitionism and the ACS. Colonizationists instigated and participated in the anti-abolitionist riots that swept the North in the mid-1830s. Many foes of slavery abandoned the ACS. Nonetheless, while no longer the main embodiment of white antislavery sentiment, colonization survived as part of the broad spectrum of ideas relating to slavery and abolition. Lincoln grew up in Kentucky and southern Indiana and then lived in central Illinois among migrants from the Upper South. These were areas where the idea of colonization enjoyed considerable support. In 1833, a local colonization society was organized at Springfield, with numerous leading citizens as members, including John T. Stuart, soon to become Lincoln's first law partner. For many white Americans, including Lincoln, colonization represented a middle ground between the radicalism of the abolitionists and the prospect of the United States existing permanently half-slave and half-free.[11]

In the 1850s, Lincoln emerged as a public spokesman for colonization. His first extended discussion of the idea came in 1852, in his eulogy after Henry Clay's death. This was delivered at a time when Lincoln's career in public office appeared to be over, so it is hard to see a political motivation for the speech. Most eulogists praised Clay as the Great Compromiser, the man who had almost single-handedly saved the Union in a series of sectional crises. Lincoln, by contrast, emphasized, indeed exaggerated, Clay's devotion to the "cause of human liberty." Lincoln hailed Clay for occupying a position between two "extremes"—those whose assaults on slavery threatened the Union and those who looked to no end to the institution. He quoted some of Clay's pro-colonization speeches and embraced Clay's idea of gradual emancipation linked with returning blacks to their "long-lost fatherland." Lincoln addressed the Illinois State Colonization Society's annual meetings in 1853 and 1855. In 1858, the year of his senate race, Lincoln's was the first name listed among the eleven members of the Society's Board of Managers.[12]

In some ways Lincoln's colonizationism proved quite different from that of others of his time. While encouraging blacks to emigrate, he never countenanced compulsory deportation. He said little about the danger of racial mixing, except when, goaded by Democrats, he declared his opposition to interracial marriage and pointed out that the more slavery expanded, the more likely it was for "amalgamation" to occur. Unlike Jefferson, Lincoln did not seem to fear a racial war if slavery were abolished, and unlike other colonizationists he expressed little interest in the Christianization of Africa. (Lincoln's own antislavery beliefs arose from democratic and free-labor convictions, not religious perfectionism.) Lincoln never spoke of free blacks as a vicious and degraded group dangerous to the stability of American society. In his 1852 eulogy, when he mentioned the "dangerous presence" in the United States, it was not free blacks, but slavery.[13]

In the mid-1850s, Thomas Jefferson supplanted Clay as Lincoln's touchstone of political wisdom. He referred repeatedly to Jefferson's belief in natural equality. Nonetheless, like Jefferson's, Lincoln's thought seemed suspended between a "civic" conception of American nationality, based on the universal principle of equality (and thus open to immigrants and, in principle, to blacks), and a racial nationalism that saw blacks as in some ways not truly American. He found it impossible to imagine the United States as a biracial society and believed that blacks would welcome the opportunity to depart for a place where they could fully enjoy their natural rights. "What I would most desire," he said in a speech in Springfield in 1858, "would be the separation of the white and black races."[14]

Springfield, when Lincoln lived there in the 1840s and 1850s, was a small city with a tiny black population. Lincoln and his wife employed at least four free black women to work in their home at one time or another, and Lincoln befriended William Florville, the city's most prosperous black resident. But unlike Garrison and other white abolitionists, Lincoln had little contact with politically active free blacks before the Civil War.

Blacks in Illinois held their first statewide conventions in the 1850s, beginning with a gathering in Chicago in 1853. Primarily aimed at organizing a movement for repeal of the state's repressive Black Laws, the conventions also spoke out against colonization. The Chicago delegates denounced "all schemes for colonizing the free colored people of the United States in Africa . . . as directly calculated to increase pro-slavery prejudice." A second convention in Alton in 1856 and a public meeting of Springfield blacks in February 1858 expressed similar views. "We believe," the Springfield gathering declared, "that the operations of the Colonization Society are calculated to excite prejudices against us, and they impel ignorant or ill disposed persons to take measures for our expulsion from the land of our nativity . . . We claim the right of citizenship in this, the country of our birth . . . We are not African." Another black convention in Chicago in August 1858 decisively defeated a resolution favoring emigration to some locale "on this continent." It is unlikely that Lincoln was unaware of these gatherings, which were reported in the Republican press, but he seems to have made no comment about them, and they did not affect his support for colonization.[15]

By the late 1850s, the American Colonization Society seemed moribund. The *New York Herald* called its annual convention an "old fogy affair." In 1859, of a black population of four million, including nearly a half-million free blacks, the ACS sent about three hundred persons to Liberia. "Can anything be more ridiculous," the *Herald* asked, "than keeping up such a society as this?" Yet at this very moment the idea of colonization was experiencing a revival within the young Republican Party. As in the days of Henry Clay, support centered in Lincoln's bailiwick—the border slave states and the lower Northwest.[16]

The most avid Republican promoters of colonization were the Blair family—the venerable Francis P. Blair, once a close adviser of President Andrew Jackson, and his sons Frank and Montgomery. They looked to Central America, not Africa, as the future homeland of black Americans and hoped that the promise of land and financial aid would make a colony attractive enough for a large number of blacks to settle there. Colonization was central to the Blairs' plan to speed the rise of the Republican Party and the progress of gradual, compensated emancipation in border states like Maryland and Missouri, where slavery was weak or in decline, since, they insisted, local whites would not accept the end of slavery without it.

The colonization movement had long been divided between those who saw it as a way of ridding the country of free blacks and others for whom it formed part of a long-term strategy for ending slavery. Despite their overt racism, the Blairs, like Henry Clay, were firmly in the latter camp. Before the Civil War, no one, except perhaps John Brown, could conceive of how to end slavery without the consent of slave owners. There was simply no constitutional way that this could be accomplished. And it seemed impossible that, in the border South at least, whites would ever consent to emancipation unless it were coupled with monetary compensation to the owners and the removal of the black population.

The Blairs made a special effort to enlist Lincoln in their cause. In April 1858, Lincoln and his partner, William Herndon, met in their law office with Frank Blair and developed a plan to promote the Republican Party in the Upper South. Two months later, in a speech on the Dred Scott decision at Springfield, Lincoln called for "the separation of the races" via colonization, adding that, while the Republican Party had not officially endorsed the idea, "a very large proportion of its members" favored it. Lincoln noted that, in biblical times, hundreds of thousands of Israelites had left Egypt "in a body." Lincoln saw colonization as part of a broader antislavery strategy aimed, initially at least, at the Upper South. Perhaps the Blairs offered a way of placing slavery on the road to "ultimate extinction," a hope Lincoln had expressed many times but without any real explanation of how it would take place.

These encounters seem to have affected both men. Visiting Illinois reinforced Frank Blair's conviction that Missouri must rid itself of slavery: "No resident of a slave state could pass through the splendid farms of Sangamon and Morgan, without permitting an enormous sigh to escape him at the evident superiority of free labor." As for Lincoln, he seems to have anticipated that gradual abolition would become a live issue in the uppermost Southern states. "We are to see the devil in these border states in 1860," Herndon wrote after he and Lincoln met with Blair in 1857. Certainly, Lincoln saw colonization as part of a strategy for eliminating slavery. Based on the surviving outline, his 1855 address to the state Colonization Society surveyed the history of slavery beginning in the fifteenth century and then went on to describe the spread of antislavery sentiment, culminating in the formation of the American Colonization Society in 1816. In the fifth debate with Douglas, Lincoln quoted Henry Clay to the effect that colonization would help prepare the way for emancipation. Well before Lincoln advanced his own program to encourage emancipation in the border states during the Civil War, Lincoln saw the region as a key battleground in the slavery controversy.[17]

Black conventions, previously all but unanimous in opposition to colonization, now engaged in heated discussions of the future of the race in the United States. Even Frederick Douglass, the nation's most prominent black leader, seemed to modify his longstanding opposition to emigration. For two decades, Douglass had reiterated his conviction that the colonization movement strengthened slavery and racism. But in January 1861, acknowledging that "the feeling in favor of emigration" had never been "so strong as now," Douglass planned a trip to Haiti. At the last minute, the trip was postponed. The Civil War had begun, portending, Douglass wrote, "a tremendous revolution in . . . the future of the colored race of the United States."[18]

The outbreak of war may have ended Douglass's flirtation with the idea, but from the beginning of his administration, Lincoln made known his support for colonization. His cabinet included three strong advocates—Attorney General Edward Bates of Missouri, Secretary of the Interior Caleb B. Smith of Indiana, and Montgomery Blair, the postmaster general. Even before fighting began, Elisha Crosby, the new minister to Guatemala, departed for his post carrying secret instructions, "conceived by old Francis P. Blair" and endorsed by Lincoln, to secure land for a colony of blacks "more or less under the protection of the U. S. Government."[19]

Chiriqui, on the Isthmus of Panama, then part of New Granada (today's Colombia), seemed to offer the most promising prospect for colonization. On April 10, 1861, as the crisis at Fort Sumter reached its climax, Lincoln met at the White House with Ambrose W. Thompson, head of the Chiriqui Improvement Company, who claimed to have acquired several hundred thousand acres of land in the province in 1855. He touted the region's suitability for a naval station because of its fine harbor and rich coal deposits, which colonized blacks could mine. Lincoln, according to Secretary of the Navy Welles, was "much taken with the suggestion" and pressed Welles to look into the matter. The secretary responded that the navy had no interest in a coaling station in Chiriqui, that there was "fraud and cheat in the affair," and that he doubted that blacks desired to become coal miners. Undeterred, Lincoln authorized his secretary of the interior to agree to a contract for "coal and privileges" in Chiriqui, which, Lincoln hoped, would not only benefit the federal government but help "to secure the removal of the negroes from this country."[20]

As the question of emancipation moved to the forefront of political debate in late 1861 and 1862, discussion of colonization also intensified. In his annual message to Congress, delivered on December 3, 1861, Lincoln urged Congress to provide funds for the colonization of slaves freed under the First Confiscation Act, as well as slaves that the border states might decide to free, and to consider acquiring new territory for the purpose. A Washington newspaper suggested that the proposed black colony be called Lincolnia. Overall, commented the Washington correspondent of the *New York Times*, the message took "the ancient ground of Henry Clay in regard to slavery . . . combined with the plan of Frank P. Blair, Jr."[21]

During the spring and summer of 1862, as Congress pressed ahead with antislavery legislation, colonization played an important part in its debates. The laws providing for abolition in the District of Columbia and the confiscation of the slaves of those who supported the Confederacy—important steps on the path toward general emancipation—both included provisions for the colonization of those willing to emigrate. During 1862, Congress appropriated a total of $600,000 to aid in the transportation of African Americans.

In Congress, the strongest support for colonization arose from border Unionists and moderate Republicans from the Old Northwest. Radical Republicans, many of whom had long defended the rights of northern free blacks, generally opposed the idea, although some were willing to go along to placate the president and the border states. Congressional and administration enactments in 1862 reflected these competing cross-currents. Even while appropriating money for colonization, Congress established schools for black children in Washington, D.C., decreed that the same legal code should apply to blacks and whites in the city, and repealed the longstanding exclusion of blacks from militia service. In November, Attorney General Bates, a strong supporter of colonization, issued an opinion affirming the citizenship of free black persons born in the country (in effect overturning the Dred Scott decision).[22]

Lincoln had never been a proponent of manifest destiny; unlike the Blairs, he did not seem interested in the prospect of an American empire in the Caribbean. But his focus in 1862 on promoting border state emancipation as a way of undermining the Confederacy reinforced the importance of colonization. According to the *New York Tribune*'s Washington correspondent, Lincoln frequently quoted the comment of Senator Garrett Davis of Kentucky that the state's Unionists "would not resist his gradual emancipation scheme if he would only conjoin it with his colonization plan." But Lincoln's proposal for federally assisted emancipation in the border went nowhere, even though in a last-ditch appeal on July 12 he assured members of Congress from border states that land could easily be obtained in Latin America for colonization and "the freed people will not be so reluctant to go."[23]

As talk of colonization increased, so did black opposition. To counteract this reluctance to emigrate, Lincoln, for the first and only time, took the idea of colonization directly to blacks. On August 14, 1862, for the first time in the history of the country, an American president received and addressed a number of black men. What Lincoln said, however, made this one of the most controversial moments of his entire career. "You and we are different races," Lincoln told the black delegation. Because of white prejudice, "even when you cease to be slaves, you are yet far removed from being placed on an equality with the white race . . . It is better for us both, therefore, to be separated." He offered a powerful indictment of slavery: "Your race are suffering in my judgment, the greatest wrong inflicted on any people." He refused to issue a similar condemnation of racism, although he also declined to associate himself with it. Racism, he said, was intractable; whether it "is right or wrong I need not discuss." Lincoln seemed to blame the black presence for the Civil War: "But for your race among us there could not be war." He offered their removal as the remedy.[24]

A stenographer was present, and Lincoln's remarks quickly appeared in the nation's newspapers, as he undoubtedly intended. The bulk of the antislavery public, black and white, along with many others, greeted the publication of Lincoln's remarks with dismay. Secretary of the Treasury Chase found the encounter shocking. "How much better," he remarked in his diary, "would be a manly protest against prejudice against color." A. P. Smith, a black resident of New Jersey, wrote the president: "Pray tell us, is our right to a home in this country less than your own, Mr. Lincoln? . . . Are you an American? So are we. Are you a patriot? So are we." Blacks considered it a "perfect outrage" to hear from the president that their presence was "the cause of all this bloodshed."[25]

Lincoln failed to consider that so powerful and public an endorsement of colonization might not only reinforce racism but encourage racists to act on their beliefs. Blacks reported that, since the publication of the president's remarks, they had been "repeatedly insulted, and told that we must leave the country." The summer of 1862 witnessed a series of violent outbreaks targeting blacks. Lincoln's meeting with the black delegation, wrote the antislavery *Chicago Tribune*, "constitutes the wide and gloomy background of which the foreground is made up of the riots and disturbances which have disgraced within a short time past our Northern cities." The "kindly" Lincoln, it went on, "does not mean all this, but the deduction is inevitable."[26]

Heedless of this reaction, Lincoln pressed the case for colonization with the cabinet. On September 23, the day after issuing the Preliminary Emancipation Proclamation (which included a reference to colonizing the freed people), he stated that he thought a treaty could be worked out with a government in West Africa or Central America "to which the Negroes could be sent." But by this time, numerous questions had arisen about the validity of the Chiriqui Company's land grant, its grandiose accounts of the region's natural resources, and the attitude of the local government. The Smithsonian Institution reported that samples of Chiriqui coal examined by a leading scientist were worthless. If loaded onto naval vessels, the coal "would spontaneously take fire." Most importantly, Central American governments had been complaining to Secretary of State William H. Seward about public discussion of colonies on their soil.[27]

In his annual message to Congress of December 1862, Lincoln reiterated his commitment to colonization. He asked for a constitutional amendment authorizing Congress to appropriate funds for the purpose, along with two others offering funds to states that provided for emancipation by the year 1900 and compensating owners of slaves who had gained freedom as a result of the war. Here again was his longstanding idea of ending slavery—gradual, compensated emancipation, coupled with colonization. But at the same time he directly addressed white racial fears, offering an extended argument as to why, if freed slaves remained in the United States, they would pose no threat to the white majority.

The December message was both a preparation of public opinion for the Emancipation Proclamation less than a month hence and a last offer to the border and Confederate states of a different path to abolition. Lincoln's scheme would have had the government issue interest-bearing bonds to be presented to slave owners, with the principal due when slavery ended in their state. He offered an elaborate set of calculations to prove that, despite the economic value of slave property—over three billion dollars, an enormous sum—the growth of the white population through natural increase and immigration would make the burden of taxation to pay off the bonds less and less onerous as time went on. Lincoln was betting that the white population would grow faster than the black—an outcome that colonization would ensure. Without colonization, Lincoln said, the black population might grow faster than the white, dramatically increasing the cost of his plan.[28]

On December 31, 1862, Lincoln signed a contract to transport blacks to Île á Vache (Cow Island), eight miles off the coast of Haiti. Attorney General Edward Bates described Bernard Kock, who had organized the scheme, to Lincoln as "an errant humbug . . . a charlatan adventurer." But the president agreed that Kock would be paid fifty dollars each for transporting five thousand blacks to Cow Island.[29]

On the next day, Lincoln issued the Emancipation Proclamation. It represented a turning point in the Civil War and in Lincoln's own views regarding slavery and race. In crucial respects, it differed markedly from Lincoln's previous statements and policies. It was immediate, not gradual, contained no mention of compensation for slave owners, and said nothing about colonization. Never before in the Western Hemisphere had a large number of slaves been emancipated without compensation. (Even Haiti eventually had to pay reparations to France for the abolition of slavery during the wars of the 1790s.) For the first time, Lincoln authorized the enrollment of black soldiers into the Union military. The proclamation set in motion the process by which, in the last two years of the war, 180,000 black men served in the Union army, playing a critical role in Union victory. It enjoined emancipated slaves to "labor faithfully for reasonable wages" in the United States.[30]

After issuing the Emancipation Proclamation, Lincoln made no further public statements about colonization. But he did not immediately abandon the idea. Early in February, Lincoln told William P. Cutler, a Radical Republican congressman from Ohio, that he was still "troubled to know what we should do with these people—Negroes—after peace came." (Cutler replied that he thought the plantations would continue to need their labor.) Throughout the spring, John P. Usher, a proponent of colonization who had succeeded Smith as secretary of the interior, continued to promote various schemes. In April, Lincoln gave John Hodge, a representative of the British Honduras Company, which was looking for black labor, permission to visit contraband camps in Virginia "to ascertain their willingness to emigrate." But Secretary of War Edwin M. Stanton refused, since the army was now recruiting able-bodied men for military service. "The mission failed," reported the *New York Times*, "and the gentleman went home."[31]

Thus, in the spring of 1863 it was Secretary Stanton, not Lincoln, who called a halt to colonization efforts. "The recent action of the War Department," Secretary Usher commented ruefully, "prevents the further emigration from the U. S. of persons of African descent for the present." Yet border Unionists clung to the idea of colonization. In a speech in the House in February 1864, Frank Blair excoriated those who wished to elevate blacks to equality with whites. He claimed that colonization was still the "humane, wise, and benevolent policy" of the president. By 1864, however, the influence of the border states was on the wane. In September, Lincoln asked Montgomery Blair to resign from the Cabinet as part of an effort to win Radical support for his re-election.[32]

The declining importance of the border was only one among many reasons why Lincoln's commitment to colonization faded in the last two years of the war. The service of black soldiers strongly affected his outlook. When the Emancipation Proclamation was issued, the black abolitionist H. Ford Douglas predicted that the progress of the war would "educate Mr. Lincoln out of his idea of the deportation of the Negro." Lincoln would come to believe that, in fighting for the Union, black soldiers had staked a claim to citizenship and political rights in the postwar world. In addition, contact with articulate black spokesmen like Frederick Douglass, Martin R. Delany (whom Lincoln called "this most extraordinary and intelligent black man"), Sojourner Truth, Bishop Daniel A. Payne of the African Methodist Episcopal Church, and representatives of the propertied, educated free black community of New Orleans seemed to broaden Lincoln's racial views. Simultaneously, the widespread interest in colonization evinced by members of Congress in 1862 had evaporated. When Congress in the spring of 1864 debated the Thirteenth Amendment abolishing slavery, no one supporting the measure promised to colonize the freed people.[33]

The fiasco at Île á Vache also contributed to the demise of colonization. Reports of destitution and unrest among the colonists soon began to filter back. It turned out that Kock had declared himself "governor," taken the emigrants' money, and issued scrip printed by himself—at a profit of 50 percent—to be the sole currency on the island. When they disembarked, the settlers found three dilapidated sheds and no medical facilities. The irate colonists soon drove Kock from the island. In February 1864, Lincoln ordered Secretary of War Stanton to send a ship to bring back the survivors. Thus ended the only colonization project actually undertaken by the Lincoln administration. The disaster convinced Secretary Usher to abandon the entire policy. As he explained to Lincoln, despite "the great importance which has hitherto been attached to the separation of the races," colonization was dead. On July 1, 1864, Lincoln's secretary John Hay noted in his diary, "I am glad that the President has sloughed off the idea of colonization."[34]

In 1863 and 1864, Lincoln for the first time began to think seriously of the role blacks would play in a postslavery world, what kind of labor system should replace slavery, and whether some blacks should enjoy the right to vote. In the Sea Islands, reformers were establishing schools for blacks and aiding them in acquiring land. In the Mississippi Valley, former slaves were being put to work on plantations. Lincoln expressed increasing interest in how these experiments fared. In August 1863, he instructed General Nathaniel P. Banks to include as part of wartime Reconstruction in Louisiana a system whereby "the two races could gradually live themselves out of their old relation to each other, and both come out better prepared for the new," mentioning especially "education for young blacks." In 1864, he privately suggested to Gov. Michael Hahn of Louisiana that the state's new constitution allow educated free blacks and black soldiers to vote. After winning a second term, Lincoln did try, one last time, at the Hampton Roads peace conference of February 1865, to revive the old idea of compensated emancipation and, it seems, alluded to the possibility of gradual abolition. He made no mention of colonization.[35]

The dream of a white America did not die in 1865, nor did black emigration efforts. But the end of slavery meant the end of colonization. It was Frederick Douglass who, during the Civil War, offered the most fitting obituary. Douglass argued that the idea of colonization allowed whites to avoid thinking about the aftermath of slavery. Only with the death of colonization could Americans begin to confront the challenge of creating an interracial democracy.[36]

As for Lincoln, his long embrace of colonization suggests that recent historians may have been too quick to claim him as a supremely clever politician who secretly but steadfastly pursued the goal embodied in the Emancipation Proclamation or as a model of political pragmatism in contrast to the fanatical abolitionists. For what idea was more utopian than this fantastic scheme? For a political pragmatist, Lincoln seriously misjudged the likelihood of the border states adopting emancipation, even when coupled with colonization, and the willingness of most black Americans to leave the country of their birth. Even more profoundly, he overestimated the intractability of northern racism as an obstacle to ending slavery. In fact, for a variety of reasons, the majority of the northern public came to accept emancipation without colonization. Perhaps the much-maligned abolitionists, who insisted that slavery could be ended with the freed people remaining in the United States, were actually more realistic.

Lincoln's embrace of colonization and eventual abandonment of the idea illustrates how he was both a product of his time and able to transcend it, which may be as good a definition of greatness as any. In his last public speech, shortly before his death, Lincoln spoke publically for the first time of suffrage for some blacks in the reconstructed South, notably the men "who serve our cause as soldiers." Rejection of colonization had been necessary before Lincoln came to advocate even partial civil and political equality for blacks. He had come a long way from the views he brought together in 1858 in *Abraham Lincoln: His Book*.[37]

RICHARD FOLLETT

Legacies of Enslavement

❧

Plantation Identities and the Problem of Freedom

MARDI GRAS DAWNED dark and overcast. In the riverfront town of Plaquemine, Louisiana, the Komical Klan of Komus orchestrated the gala parade. Focusing on the return of African American workers to the cane fields of Louisiana, the 1880 carnival celebrated the restoration of white rule over the land and laborers of the sugar country. The Knights of the Klan ostentatiously began the parade, followed by a band of minstrels. Next, a half-simian, half-human "man-monkey" emerged to entertain the crowd. Surrounding these racially defined figures dashed a troop of impish monkeys who served the "fat boys" who marched with them. "The colored couple on their return from Kansas," however, received the loudest cheer. Dilapidated, impoverished, and in their rags, the couple were literally limping home after their failed attempt to secure landed independence in the West. Carnivalesque in nature, the Klan's theatrics reflected the racial aspirations of white southerners who idealized black deference and who mused nostalgically on their mastery over those who toiled in the cane fields. How white southerners, and in particular Louisiana's sugar-planting elite, perceived of enslaved and free labor and how they attempted to control the image and reality of free labor are the principal topics of this essay. It, furthermore, assesses the multiple impediments black Americans faced in securing their freedom and considers how the material and ideological inheritance associated with plantation slavery shaped and limited the parameters of African American freedom in the mid-nineteenth century.[1]

Louisiana's sugar country proved unique in several ways. In the first instance, whereas tenancy and sharecropping emerged as the principal labor arrangement across the cotton states, in the sugar country, wages dominated labor relations and a proletarianized labor force emerged. Second, in distinct contrast to the rest of the U.S. South, where planters subdivided their estates into small plots for peasant production, the plantation mode on Louisiana's sugar estates proved singularly resilient from the 1850s to the 1880s. Third, sugar production developed on a semi-industrial scale. Unlike cotton, tobacco, or rice (albeit to a lesser extent), where tasks could be conducted by families or small groups, cane farming required mass field labor to plant, cultivate, and harvest the canes. In the semi-mechanized sugarhouse, steam-powered mills crushed the eight-foot-tall canes and extracted the sucrose-rich juice. Skilled workers then evaporated the juice in a series of open kettles before the sugar granulated.[2]

Under slavery, a plantation system based on large capital-intensive estates and gang labor developed, and this organizational system endured through Reconstruction. To preserve the large labor crews upon which sugar production hinged, postbellum planters experimented with a variety of wage labor systems, contracting annually and seasonally with freedpeople and migrant workers. Although the promise of landed proprietorship never faded from the horizons of former slaves (who constituted the majority of cane hands in the decades following emancipation), freedpeople in the sugar parishes necessarily paid greater attention to the question of wages, perquisites, and the length of the working week than did their peers elsewhere in the South. Utilizing their collective force in the workplace to wrestle adequate wages and terms from their employers, black cane workers vigorously contested the terms and conditions of free labor. As historians John Rodrigue and Rebecca Scott demonstrate, in the fields, sugar factories, and polling booths, former slaves also asserted their citizenship rights by advancing a political agenda that extended from grassroots Republican activism to labor organization in the 1880s.[3]

The crowd who gathered for the Klan's Mardi Gras pastiche chose to think or remember differently. There, footloose and unmanageable labor underwent a transformation. In the eyes of the crowd, if not always in reality, vigorous black resistance gave way to racially soothing stereotypes, images of servitude that could be controlled, confined, and ultimately mastered. The meek-mute returnees from Kansas (members of a community who fled the region in the late 1870s) seemed to exercise no agency, at least to those who jeered at the parade. In their eyes, black labor appeared abject, illegitimate, inferior, and dependent on white patronage and power. The returnees also seemed to lack the basic credentials for citizenship (liberty, property, self-control, and a public voice). Relegated to the social, economic, and racial base of southern society, the returning cane hands appeared to be little more than servants—a lower order in a stratified social system based on white supremacy and black subordination. The chattering monkey and fat boys confirmed this image, suggesting that African Americans remained genetically and psychologically ill-suited to govern others. The man-monkey similarly conformed to midcentury racial assumptions. Darting among the crowd, the hybrid-simian clearly followed no rules, his lawlessness refusing the ordered, hierarchical structure of the parade. Behind his mask, the man-monkey was a powerful symbol of the irrepressible and insurrectionary nature of African American males and evidence, it seemed, that black men and dark apes derived from the same genetic pool. The man-monkey, however, fathomed ethnographic racism still further, for his frenetic movement gestured toward a lasciviousness that plumbed three centuries of white racial thought about black sexuality. Ascribing both indolence and insurrection to the black figures who literally and figuratively danced within their minds, white southerners applauded the assertive masculinity of the Klan and the restoration of white Democratic rule after a decade of black Republican dominance.[4]

In reality, the transition from slave to free labor in the postemancipation South proved infinitely more turbulent than that depicted in the Mardi Gras parade. Still, for sugar planters who faced wage demands, strike action, and black political pressure, the concept of securing pliable and dependent labor remained especially alluring. The planter class's search for dominion over those they once owned proved equally arresting. As historian Thomas Holt observes, the "problem of freedom" resonated throughout post-emancipation societies. For the recently emancipated, the "problem" was to reconcile their economic and political liberties within the emerging free labor structure. Former slaveholders viewed the "problem" differently. Having articulated the most comprehensive defense of chattel bondage of any New World slave society and then declared political independence to defend the institution, American slaveholders responded to slave emancipation with a mix of anger, resentment, and apprehension. Those sentiments grew with the enfranchisement of former slaves in 1867. With the mantle of slaveholding mastery stripped away, southern planters nevertheless strove to reassert their command over the work crews and address what they euphemistically called the "labor problem." Packed within the labor issue, however, lay a more generic and fundamental concern—the extent to which African Americans could exercise their economic and social freedom and the extent to which planters could assert their control over labor.[5]

The postbellum labor question and the problem of freedom, however, were sharply influenced by the history of slavery. Indeed, just as enslaved people entered free society with skills and attitudes hewn from bondage, slaveholders approached freedom with their own values, experiences, and ideologies rooted to a history of racial and class exploitation. These ideological, material, and experiential "legacies of enslavement" proved exceptionally durable and shaped the contours of post-emancipation society across the rural South. In particular, the densely racialized and gendered values of plantation slavery did not disappear with the constitutional amendments of Reconstruction. As historian Thavolia Glymph observes, former slaveholders invested in and were "riveted to (socially, psychologically, and economically) the existence of a subordinated race." Although freedpeople attempted to de-couple this narrative by affirming their rights and identities as individuals and citizens, southern whites conflated blackness with slavery (or dependency at the very least), and they retained trenchant assumptions on the immutability of race. Nowhere was this truer than in Louisiana's sugar country. In fact, the resilience of the plantation mode in Louisiana's sugar country ensured that the rhetoric and practices of white slaveholding power endured tenaciously. So, too, did antebellum assumptions about racialized and deferential labor. To this extent, the sugar elite were not unlike other postbellum planters where traditional orthodoxies prevailed. But as this essay indicates, these legacies of enslavement haunted the sugar region in significant ways and shadowed attempts by former slaves and enslavers to forge a society built on free labor following the Civil War. African Americans, in particular, addressed the "problem of freedom" head on—striking, withdrawing their labor, and reshaping plantation life to advance their economic and political interests. Planters, by contrast, could not remake the postbellum world in their own image, but in their attempts to confine African Americans to a social and economic underclass, they revealed as much about the frustration of power as about its successful exercise. In so doing, they addressed a central postemancipation problem. How, and in what ways, would the material, cultural, and ideological imprint of slavery continue to shape rural life and patterns of local power long after the institution of racial slavery was abolished?[6]

"Condition of servitude"

For much of the nineteenth century, black workers toiled in the cane fields of Louisiana to raise and harvest the annual sugar crop. Cultivated along the lower reaches of the Mississippi River, cane sugar production expanded during the early nineteenth century and by 1850 some 125,000 enslaved African Americans toiled on 1,500 estates across southern Louisiana. Those slaves produced almost all the cane sugar manufactured in the United States, supplying approximately half of the American demand for sugar. Buoyed by federal tariffs, planters invested heavily in land, labor, and machinery to increase production. On average, large sugar planters owned 110 slaves, 1,600 acres of land, and machinery valued between $14,000 and $27,000 (five times the mechanical capital of the largest cotton planters). These cane lords produced three-quarters of the sugar and owned two-thirds of the land and slaves in south Louisiana. By 1861, sugar planters owned some of the largest slaveholding units in the country. As America went to war, they produced more than 450,000 hogsheads of sugar. It was the largest and last sugar crop made entirely with slave labor and the crowning moment of the antebellum sugar masters.[7]

Cane farmers, nevertheless, faced a series of acute ecological constraints. In the first instance, cane sugar did not thrive naturally in Louisiana. The threat of ice damage dictated that slaves planted the canes in January and began harvesting them in mid-October. From that point, the annual grinding season was a race against time as planters drove their crews to cut the canes and manufacture the sugar before the first killing frosts descended. To address these meteorological constraints, planters held speed at an absolute premium. As Timothy Flint observed, the managerial order resembled "a garrison under military discipline." Everything, he observed, is "managed by system." By the late 1850s, planters intensified the labor order still further by investing in a highly capital-intensive plantation system. They purchased steam-powered sugar mills to grind cane swiftly, dragooned gang labor, and synchronized field operations with those in the millhouse. Above all, they acquired thousands of enslaved male laborers (aged 18–28). Applying the terms "likely, choice, of consequence" for the muscular young men deemed strong enough for sugar work, planters fashioned an idealized and racially marked body for sugar. With longstanding gendered assumptions in mind about the relative merits of male and female labor in cane sugar production, planters discriminated by age and sex to form physically robust, male-dominated work crews. As the *Daily Picayune* staunchly declared: "The two great staples of the South—cotton and sugar, to which add rice—can only be profitably raised by the negro, and by him, *ex necessitate rei*, in a condition of servitude."[8]

To compel the slaves to labor at the metered cadence of the steam age, planters utilized the whip and incentives, particularly during the harvest season, when the working day extended long into the night.

Slowdowns at harvest-time proved hazardous for the crop, and both planters and enslaved people understood this fact. To diminish these risks, planters introduced financial incentives and crop-over perquisites, including overwork payment, harvest bonuses, and cash for the produce of the slaves' provision grounds. When backed up with whipping, planters hoped these measures might induce efficient and productive labor. Slaves viewed payment differently. By employing their power at the center of production or threatening to withhold it, cane workers recognized that they could secure a modest (albeit insecure) income for expenditure on personal and household items. By contrast, planters declared these payments to be gifts or cash benefits granted at the discretion and munificence of the master. Season-specific paternalism of this type did not preclude violence (far from it), but it provided slaveholders with an opportunity to cloak self-interest with the illusion of idealized mastery, and it linked the economic well-being of the slave (individually and collectively) to the success of the planter. For those in the field gangs, such payment did not carry the ideological clutter of paternalism and mastery; rather, it was a convenient way to put money in their pockets and grounds for fierce contestation should planters fail to honor these customary practices.[9]

"Slaves made free are comparatively worthless"

The Civil War decoupled the planters' narrative. Soon after the first federal warships steamed up the Mississippi in April 1862, slaves began fleeing to Union lines. Those who remained on the estates demanded pay for their labor or simply refused to work. As planter Effingham Lawrence observed, the slaves were "in a state of mutiny." With the harvest season approaching and with talk of "insurrection, rebellion, and midnight murder" circulating, the cane workers pressed home their advantage, demanding ten dollars a month for their labor, erecting a gallows in the quarters, and promising to hang the managers on Lawrence's estate. Overseer J. A. Randall concluded pithily, on the dissolution of plantation authority, "so it goes, slaves made free are comparatively worthless." Lawrence nevertheless intervened personally, promising the hands a "handsome present" if they resumed work. Ultimately making a one-off payment of twenty-five hundred dollars (equivalent to more than twenty dollars per head) to those who returned to their posts, Lawrence refused to recognize the payment as a wage. It was a gift for "good conduct" more than remuneration for the work conducted.[10]

Lawrence chose to exorcize the tumultuous events of the summer with a wishful statement on his mastery. On most estates, however, a patchwork of waged and semi-waged relations emerged, which roughly followed the contours of the free labor program instituted by Union Generals Benjamin Butler and Nathaniel Banks. Although exempt from the terms of the Emancipation Proclamation, the Banks-Butler program ensured that slaves in the occupied sugar parishes returned to the cane fields. There, they labored in gangs (six days a week, ten hours a day) in return for wages (paid in cash individually or collectively to the workers as one-twentieth of the crop). They would, moreover, reside within the quarters and cultivate their provision grounds much as they had done under slavery. Union regulations required planters to furnish food and medicine, provide for dependents, and inflict no corporal punishment. In return, federal authority buttressed plantation rule. Military guards preserved order and returned vagrants to their employers. As Nathaniel Banks observed in February 1864, "the revolution has altered its tenure, but not its law." The *New York Times* concurred, noting that "freedom and slavery have ... got so jumbled up ... that it is hard to tell which is the boss." President Lincoln adopted more conciliatory language but nevertheless described Banks's regime as a "temporary arrangement," an apprenticeship program that offered slaveholders the means to regulate labor and rejuvenate the plantation economy.[11]

In return for this interim, albeit backward-looking inducement, the president hoped that the sugar elite (who had been reticent to leave the safety of U.S. tariff protection in 1861) might accept freedom for the slaves and support Louisiana's readmission to the Union. These were not unreasonable expectations. Most sugar planters supported the Whig Party and its commercially protectionist platform during the 1840s. Many, in fact, had voted for Unionist candidates in 1860 but seceded when they believed slavery to be under mortal threat. But with planters uneasily recognizing that "slavery is dead [even if its] spirit still lives," Lincoln dangled the prospect of regulation (though not enslavement) of black workers before the sugar elite. With these inducements, Lincoln hoped that sugar planters might form part of the "tangible nucleus" of Unionists he was attempting to organize in Louisiana.[12]

Political expediency aside, the free labor order grafted what planters deemed to be serviceable precedent onto the rudiments of waged work. Indeed, to Thomas P. Knox, who toured the occupied parishes, the distinctions between the "old and new systems of management" appeared to be minimal. In fact, the "spirit" of slavery seemed very much alive. Planters continued to assume that it was their right to command African American labor at will, they believed workers should live in the closely regulated quarters, and they considered it their prerogative to intervene in personal matters. While planters jealously guarded these principles, their understanding of individual and state power began to change. In particular, the presence of the Union army and the regulatory orders of the Republican state transformed established patterns of locally rooted power and the petty sovereignty of plantation rule. Some masters undoubtedly found these new realities uncomfortable, though the majority recognized that state power could be harnessed in familiar directions. Written in concert with prominent sugar planters, Banks's regulatory orders accordingly empowered army officers to reestablish staple production and provided state-sanctioned regulations for racial and labor control.[13]

The fact that Union regulations reinforced planter power did not go unnoticed among New Orleans's prominent black community. The African American press lambasted Banks as a false prophet and his labor system as "mitigated bondage" for "mock freedom." Calling for the dissolution of the plantation complex and the partition of land among its cultivators, the *New Orleans Tribune* acidly observed, "It is true that the law calls him a freeman, but any white man, subjected to such restrictions and humiliating prohibitions, will certainly call himself a slave." The "old organs of the slavery system," the *Tribune* tellingly concluded, "remain in position."[14]

Looking down the other end of the telescope, sugar magnates watched with anger and despondency as the old mechanisms of control gave way. One former mistress indignantly observed: "We are such miserable dogs, we deserve to be slaves. It would have been better to have fought until we were exterminated than live to endure such ills as are put upon us. The hardest thing for one to realize is the freedom of the negroes." She was not alone in her incredulity. Without the physical and psychological power of mastery, an unprecedented order beckoned. The language of equality, citizenship, and social justice began to circulate among the African American community, impelling some black men to enlist in the Union army and wage war against their former owners. Others attempted to shake off the worst excesses of white plantation rule. As one former slave plainly remarked, "Give us the opportunity to do what we *can* do, and do it for *ourselves* . . . all we ask, all I want for my people, is to be rid for ever of MASTERISM."[15]

Masterism was not easily shrugged off. In fact, most planters recoiled at the thought of equality in contract, and they sought to reestablish their authority through familiar and tested forms of plantation management. Planter William Minor, for instance, experienced the almost complete collapse of his authority during the war years. Even while he fumed that "the wish of the Negro is now the white man's law," Minor could divorce himself from neither his antebellum roots nor his predilection for highly intimate management. As the veteran slaveholder observed, his waged employees "must be got back to the old way of doing business by degrees."[16]

Minor, however, could not turn the clock back. Gang work advanced sporadically with former slaves halting work to attend political meetings or simply disobeying the dozens of rules that regulated life on Minor's estates. Work began late in the morning; women absented themselves from work (claiming Friday and the weekend for themselves); others proved insolent or ran off. Theft increased, as did the destruction of property. As former slaves exerted their power over the means of production, Minor's rule fractured still further. The withdrawal of black labor left the sugar lord perplexed and livid; not only did it overturn antebellum precedent, but it struck Minor as an unacceptable reversal of wage labor, too. In return for contract and wages, Minor expected his workers to labor reliably and faithfully. But as he swiftly discovered, wages did not compel the kind of stability and dependability he associated with slave labor. The share system seemed equally problematic. Like other planters who had used harvest bonuses previously, Minor believed that shares might induce hard labor and encourage self-policing against laggards within the crew. The reverse, however, occurred. As he bristled in his diary, the workers labored only four hours a day, yet they expected food, housing, clothing, clean water, wood, and medical care "and are very violent if told they do not work enough." Worse still, the laborers refused to reserve a portion of cane for seeding next year's crop. Instead, they ground all the cane, maximized the yield, and claimed their share (one-twentieth of the crop). Watching antebellum precedent turned upon its head, Minor seethed: "A man had as well burn in purgatory as attempt to work a sugar plantation under present circumstances."[17]

"The difficulty," Minor explained in April 1865, "has been to control the labor." Cane sugar, he recalled, "is an artificial crop . . . & we are obliged to do certain things at certain times." On his three estates, this structured regimen had broken down and with it, he concluded, so had morale among the workers. Wife beating, fighting, gambling, and excessive drinking symbolized the malaise associated with emancipation. In Minor's world, the dissolution of plantation discipline triggered a chain reaction: laborers allegedly became "demoralized"; this, in turn, infected the quarters, where purportedly stable families began to quarrel. From Minor's perspective, social and agricultural order were mutually dependent; instability in one led to fault lines in the other. For this reason, control over labor necessitated control over housing, family life, and the private affairs of those who resided in the quarters. But with his workers declining contracts, uprooting to Natchez, moving to other estates, or joining collective labor companies that African Americans established on abandoned estates, Minor could see that the fabric of rural paternalism was fraying quickly. No longer would the terms "sound or first-rate or fancy" adequately describe slave laborers; in their place, Minor jotted "very insolent, idle and insolent, insolent to a degree, and little insolent" on the payment records. With his mastery crumbling and his confidence in free black labor dissolving, Minor scowled, "The negro is certainly the greatest hypocrite and best actor in the world."[18]

"As near a state of bondage as possible"

Union victory in the Civil War delivered a crushing blow to William Minor and the prewar planter elite. By 1865 sugar production slumped to levels not known since the 1790s. Fewer than two hundred plantations remained in operation, while the value of Louisiana's sugar industry collapsed sevenfold. Wartime confiscation and the depreciation of property weakened planters still further. With neither the capital nor the labor to maintain the levee system, landlords watched in horror as the Mississippi and its tributaries burst their banks in the spring and summer of 1865. High water in 1867, 1868, and 1871 inundated cane fields and flooded some of the richest real estate in nineteenth-century America. Amid the general devastation, slaveholders felt the revolutionary impact of the Thirteenth Amendment most keenly. The abolition of slavery liberated more than 120,000 slaves in the sugar-producing parishes, forcibly replacing slavery with free labor. It eliminated without compensation $100 million of private capital from the portfolios of the sugar planters and abolished the enforced dominion of master over slave. The "grooves in which society had run" were so altered that it seemed like five hundred years had passed, so considerable were the distinctions between the old South and the new. For slaveholders who understood their liberty as power, and in particular the power associated with slaveholding mastery, emancipation proved devastating. As one planter exclaimed, "What a difference between the present and past . . . *freedom* has come, *contentment* and *happiness* have fled!" Shorn from their slaveholding roots and thoroughly dislocated by emancipation, planters stumbled into the new order declaring, "I don't know what to do or how to act." No laws regulated free society with the discipline of bondage, the racial etiquette of deferential submission no longer held sway, and federal jurisdiction replaced the sovereignty of independent mastery.[19]

The crippling effect of civil war and emancipation cast a decade-long shadow over the plantation elite. But despite the climate of "general paralysis," the widespread indebtedness of planters, and the limited availability of credit (which dampened any enthusiasm among planters to modernize the industry), sugar farming continued. For landlords who depended on gang work, the availability and tractability of labor proved the fundamental problem. Worker intransigency fueled dewy-eyed romanticism for the antebellum past, yet their contempt for "chronic loafers and idlers" reflected the planters' search for stability in a world turned upside down. Speaking bluntly about his desire to restore the prewar order, one overseer raged, "I think God intended the niggers to be slaves; we have the Bible for that . . . Now since man has deranged God's plan," he snapped, "I think the best we can do is to keep 'em as near a state of bondage as possible."[20]

With theological racism and slaveholding annulled, planters attempted to resurrect their authority with the passage of the black codes. These restrictive laws (passed under Johnsonian Reconstruction) represented a fundamental rejection of emancipation and employed state power as a surrogate for slavery. Drawn up by prominent sugar planter Duncan F. Kenner, Louisiana's black codes envisioned a plantation system modeled on antebellum precedent. They bound workers to the plantations, immobilized those who sought to quit, and silenced free speech and assembly. The planters' regulatory dream, however, swiftly turned to anguished nightmare. The 1866 Civil Rights Act effectively nullified the black codes, while the Fourteenth Amendment empowered the federal government to protect the rights of all citizens. Although Johnson attempted to stem the legislative challenge, Republicans passed the Reconstruction Act in March 1867. Under congressional stewardship, each state granted civil equality and electoral rights to African Americans and assured them of equal justice before the law.[21]

The 1868 Louisiana Constitution incorporated these radical principles. For leading planters who watched the state altér from ally to adversary, the early years of congressional Reconstruction seemed nothing short of revolutionary. Meeting the Republican challenge head-on, white conservatives cohered behind the Democratic Party and associated vigilante groups who intimidated and murdered newly enfranchised African American voters in the months preceding the federal elections of November 1868. Their pressure paid off, and the black-dominated Republican vote collapsed in Louisiana. Still, despite their violent opposition, southern vigilantes could not prevent the election of Republican candidate Ulysses Grant as president. If Grant's victory seemed illegitimate to Louisiana Democrats, the gubernatorial administration of Illinois-born Henry Clay Warmoth (1868–72) appeared equally abhorrent. In reality, Warmoth proved relatively conciliatory to the white upper classes. Still, for sugar planters, the factionalism and allegations of corruption during Warmoth's term symbolized the malaise of Republicanism. Although African Americans constituted less than one-third of the state legislators, it seemed like a deluge for most whites. Following Warmoth's impeachment in 1872, P. B. S. Pinchback (the son of an emancipated slave and her former master) served as acting governor. Planters bridled at these political and social changes. They considered Radical rule an abomination and the Republican governors wholly illegitimate.[22]

Former slaves, by contrast, emerged from bondage with several key lessons intact. Having secured a small, albeit fragmentary, income as slaves, freedpeople were broadly familiar with payment structures, and they also understood how to levy their power at the heart of the sugar economy to maximize terms. Those who had received bonus payments under slavery understood deferred payment arrangements and, although antebellum practices were fundamentally different (in law, practice, and culture) from waged contracts, former slaves proved relatively quick converts to the free labor order. Having honed their negotiating skills under late antebellum slavery and sharpened them still further during the federal free labor program, African Americans were relatively well positioned to secure decent terms in the workplace in the immediate postwar years. Stripped of their power to bestow or deny, planters by contrast "required more teaching . . . than even the Negroes before they could adapt themselves to the new system."[23]

In fact, the new order conciliated both planters and freedmen. Even the Freedmen's Bureau, which Congress established in March 1865 to oversee the free labor program, combined wartime precedent with the waged order. Bureau agents assumed neutrality in wage negotiations, though their work benefited both parties. Former slaves acquired a living wage, while planters secured a relatively stable group of laborers for the agricultural year. Customarily, workers contracted for the year in return for monthly wages of fifteen dollars. Landlords additionally provided rations, accommodation, garden plots, and use of the landlord's tools (as established under the Butler-Banks system). During the harvest, employers increased monthly wages and paid additional laborers on a daily basis. Planters paid wages in arrears monthly (though occasionally weekly) to regular employees. They nevertheless held back half of the wages until the end of the year. This ensured that workers would not break their contract midyear. Reflecting their age and gender bias, planters paid women about two-thirds of a comparable male wage and they similarly scaled back payment to those classified as second- or third-class hands. Those with experience and particular "merit," such as skilled engineers, sugar makers, and millhouse operatives, commanded higher pay.[24]

Under this waged system, production began to recover (albeit modestly). Planters nevertheless complained vociferously about the wage labor system and the availability of labor. Disgorging their anger in personal papers and local newspaper columns, the planters' invective masked a deeper emotional scar, namely their incapacity to control workers with the kind of direct authority they once jealously guarded. In particular, the freedmen's defiance in the cane fields, the temporary retraction of labor, the reclaiming of personal time, and the "skulking about" off-plantation irritated the landlords. Surliness, political activism, and the taking of holidays similarly grated with planters more used to dictating than being dictated to. Like many of his class, Paul

DeClouet was incensed when his employees took holidays by right. The equality implicit in such actions appalled DeClouet, who raged in his diary: "Holy Friday! No work this morning the negroes being too pious to violate such holiness *by work*, but not too much so to go and harpoon fish." Channeling pro-slavery sentiment into postbellum racism, DeClouet hoped that the "filthy Yankee and dirty negroe will be hauled back to their natural places of inferiority." A committed Confederate, DeClouet proved equally disparaging on July 4th. The field hands, he reported, celebrated their own independence and the national holiday with "idleness." These violations of plantation discipline infuriated DeClouet; they epitomized "the want of *reliable*" and "*efficient* labor" that landlords persistently grumbled about. Especially troubling was the freedmen's inclination to "move about" in search of better wages or seek a more lenient manager at the end of the year-long contract.[25]

DeClouet's anger reflected his incapacity to regulate labor with the surety bondage once afforded. But his concerns over the relative balance of power in labor relations were based in reality, too. By withholding their labor, breaking contract, or relocating elsewhere, freedpeople contributed to shortfalls in the local labor market. Job opportunities in nearby New Orleans lured some workers away, but it was the prospect of securing higher wages on neighboring estates that prompted cane hands to move elsewhere. To secure an adequate number of workers, planters competed with one another, enticing laborers away with promises of better wages and terms. Self-interest trumped any illusion of class alliance as "needy and delinquent planters" swarmed like "hornets" during the January hiring market. Although industry-wide commentators urged planters to fix wages and regulate "the labor question," landlords remained divided. Intense competition and "mutual antagonism" among planters enabled workers to demand higher pay rates locally and across the industry. Unsurprisingly, planters bridled at the wage demands, noting that cane hands earned considerably more in wages and nonmonetary compensation than did other workers throughout the country. They considered fifteen dollars a month plus rations too generous, particularly given their indebtedness. As one landlord exclaimed in 1874, "The negroes are the only ones who have made a living since the War." Worse still, "they want their own terms and conditions," another complained.[26]

Planters occasionally collaborated to set wages, define terms, and stem "enticement," but these efforts were in vain. Monthly wage rates increased from $10 to $12 in the late 1860s to between $13 and $18 in the mid-1870s. Harvest pay (in cash) similarly rose in the early 1870s to between 75¢ and $1.25 per day and to 50¢ for night work. When pay was not forthcoming, problems escalated. Since former slaves associated settling up with justice and equity, delaying payment provoked the workers and made them less likely to contract for the following season. On Edward Gay's estate, for instance, freedpeople upped the stakes when estate manager R. J. Smith failed to pay the workers. Laying claim to the product of their labor as collateral, the workers refused to ship the sugar until their wage demands were met. Fearful for his life, Smith rushed to New Orleans to secure one thousand dollars cash for the expectant workers. He was right to be anxious, as the laborers' wages formed a lien on the planter's crop. Legally obliged to settle their accounts and dangerously buffeted by the workers' wage demands, farmers like Smith dwelled less on their own shortcomings and instead blamed their difficulties upon the "fickle disposition" and "uncertainty of negro labor."[27]

Like many of their class, postbellum planters and managers such as Smith commented negatively on the character and personality of former slaves. Free labor implied equity, where the individual understood the value of his labor and sold it accordingly. Having contracted, however, planters believed strikes, slowdowns, or loafing to be evidence of the freedman's indolent, feckless character and his incapacity to grasp the fundamentals of waged employment. Judging African Americans "improvident and naturally wanting in energy," planters concluded that former slaves could not be transformed into a docile and productive working class. Nor could they be normalized to sober, rational, and responsible labor. Relegating the freedman to the margins of the waged order, planters sweepingly concluded, "Upon this class of laborer but little can be reckoned." Another bluntly added, "We have serious doubts about Cuffy as a planter."[28]

Such reservations drew upon pro-slavery rhetoric and the belief in the innate biological inferiority of African Americans in the United States and elsewhere. Writers who had commented negatively on slave emancipation in the British West Indies thirty years previously had focused expressly on the social dislocation of abolition and the attendant collapse of plantation agriculture. As James Shannon argued, without the "guardianship of the white race," Caribbean blacks degenerated into a dissolute, idle, and indolent people who were ill-qualified for freedom and incapable of sustained field labor. Racist sentiments like these found a national audience, too. New Hampshire Democrat Edmund Burke announced in 1856 that the "voice of history" sustained the degeneration thesis. Only the institution of slavery and the "directing mind" of the planter class, pro-slavery advocates argued, prevented racial degeneration of the type described and the haunting prospect of black rebellion.[29]

After emancipation, former slaveholders reworked these arguments into a narrative of black decline. Thus, when freedpeople refused to contract, planters concluded there must be "something wrong" with them. It appeared they suffered from a kind of disease, not unlike the alleged medical inflictions that reputedly caused slaves to abscond with or destroy property. Planters who utilized scientific racism to explain slave disease found many of the biological and sociological explanations for black inferiority rehashed in new ethnographic studies published in the immediate postwar years. As journalist Edward Pollard concluded, "the true status of the Negro" rested on the (biological, philosophical, and moral) "fact" of his inferiority. Attacking the concept of equality implicit in the Fifteenth Amendment, John Van Evrie concluded that African Americans were ill-suited for freedom and ill-equipped for the rights of citizenship. Racist apologists extended this analogy to suggest that African Americans would wither and die in freedom. Charles Darwin's conclusions that "the civilized races will . . . replace the savage races" gained traction in the postwar southern mind. Above all, the concept of racial extinction explained black degeneration as a natural and inevitable phenomenon. Without the coercive power of slavery, one Massachusetts-born mistress observed, the entire black race had become "treacherous, difficult, and unreliable." Trapped in a declension narrative that reduced the black male almost to savagery, she concluded that demoralized African Americans would soon become an "extinct race."[30]

When African Americans refused such negative racial marking, planters responded uneasily. Independent black labor appeared particularly subversive and insurrectionary. Those apocalyptic fears began in the plantation quarters. Like their enslaved predecessors, postbellum cane workers resided in clapboard cabins arrayed along narrow streets to the rear of the plantation mansion. Under slavery, the co-location of the cabins aided regulation and the close, direct supervision of racial bondage. Slaveholders also hoped that, in their plain, indeterminate, and monochrome uniformity, the quarters might remind their residents that power led directly from the mansion or "big" house back to the cabins. With emancipation, freedpeople across the rural South actively sought to demolish the quarters and live in individual cabins far from the prying eye of the landlord. In Louisiana's sugar region, by contrast, the quarters remained. The Banks program established this precedent and included the provision of plantation housing within the wage-labor contract. These principles endured into the postwar years. For landlords, the advantages of the quarters roughly equated to the organizational benefits accrued under slavery. More significantly still, by ensuring that former slaves occupied the very same cabins and garden plots as their enslaved predecessors, landlords actively hoped to perpetuate the dependent social relations that slavery had sought to inculcate. The ordered cabins did not symbolize autonomy, independence, and the rights of citizenship; far from it, for landlords they stood as "bare geometric expressions" of the planters' sway and as cultural and ideological artifacts of bondage. As under slavery, African Americans subverted the planter's notional and ideologically constructed landscape by utilizing the quarters—much like the gangs as organizational nodes for political and labor mobilization—but from the sightline of the planter's residence, the rigid lines of workers' cabins engraved dependence and inferiority onto the plantation landscape.[31]

Yet, as former slaves gathered and gossiped, argued and laughed, this narrative unraveled. The serenity and silence that slaveholders associated with plantation pastoralism (or quietude) gave way to impromptu assemblies, shouts, religious meetings, and political organization. Verbal encounters at the plantation commissary, where former slaves traded the produce of their garden plots, similarly challenged the social and acoustic order. Every credit and debit line told its own story as freedpeople laid claim to their economic independence in thousands of transactions at the commissary. Be they amiable or replete with venom and the pointing of accusatory fingers, these trans- and interactions nevertheless represented a visible and audible challenge to the idealized land- and soundscape of plantation rule. Angry shouts from the levee crest, political meetings at the sugar mill, secret gatherings in the canebrakes, impertinence in the cane fields, and glaring eyes from cabin stoops represented fraught encounters that punctured the audibly quiet paternalism that slaveholders associated with bondage.[32]

Slavery, of course, had never been bucolic. In fact, it had been abusive, violent, and thoroughly exploitative. Planters nevertheless exorcized such memories. They associated slavery with social order, loyalty, and benevolence. When freedpeople challenged this ideological construct and threatened long-established idioms of racial difference, hierarchy, dependence, and even silence, planters responded alarmingly and aggressively. Emancipation and the dissolution of bondage, in particular, triggered fears of insurrection, insubordination, and intimidation among planters and neighboring whites. Anxieties peaked during the Christmas insurrection scare of 1865 but remained ever-present. The onset of Radical rule inflamed white anxieties still further as groups of freedmen armed with shotguns, pistols, and clubs swaggered through towns. Newspaper editors fueled the tension, reporting eye-popping tales and "diabolical outrages" launched by "conspiracies" of black Republicans. Drawing upon the rhetoric and paranoia of slave revolt, editors ratcheted up white fear and anger in equal measure. In Saint Martinville, a rural town made famous by Longfellow's dreamy poem *Evangeline*, black political protest triggered alarm among local whites as the violently contested November 1868 elections neared. Street processions of black Republicans, shouting and hollering at passers-by, followed by riders galloping through the streets and angry threats to torch the town, visibly and audibly shattered white authority. Black political activism on the plantations triggered still greater fear among landlords. When freedmen began drilling openly, converting sugar houses into barracks, one correspondent shrieked, "It is a Radical hell . . . and they have their Radical satans there."[33]

Although white Louisianans frequently blamed northern white agitators for Republican insurgency, thereby denying free will to black activists, African American militias terrified them. Swiftly drawing parallels between their own condition and the 1865 Morant Bay rebellion, where freedpeople rose against the Jamaican elite, planters warned, "Let the negroes and white men beware." To many planters, the disordered politics and outright dangers of black rule overwhelmingly demonstrated that African American citizenship represented a perilous threat. So, too, did black office holding. "God forgive them," wrote Paul DeClouet, after attending a political barbecue in New Iberia. The mobbish black delegates who masqueraded under the mantle of legitimate political authority looked like "monkies attired for a show . . . we got home fatigued and disgusted." For DeClouet, the barbecue, the street demonstration, and the "idleness" of the cane hands were inexorably linked. In his world, as in the worlds of many white southerners, political, labor, and social disorder represented the illegitimacy of emancipation, the bankruptcy of free labor, and the depravity of Republican rule.[34]

"They won't do"

"Leave the negro to his fate," trumpeted the West Baton Rouge *Sugar Planter* in February 1866. Predicting a war between the races and the "annihilation" of African Americans, editor Henry Hyams joined the chorus of opinion in the immediate postwar years advocating the replacement of free black labor with white tenant farmers and immigrant labor. Neither ultimately sufficed, though landlords were initially enthusiastic about both groups. Indeed, to local boosters, white farming appeared like a panacea and a means to resolve the labor problem. "Let the doubting Thomases ruminate," one Plaquemine native declared, white tenant farmers would restore land values, recover abandoned estates, and increase sugar production.[35]

Having tested the "doubtful character" of black field labor, some planters calculated that savings could be made with tenancy. In so doing, they freighted whiteness with frugality and blackness with indolence. With tenants, there were no overseers to pay, no commission merchants, no nonproducing dependents to maintain, and no "drones" avoiding work on the plantation. They seemed more efficient, too. As one commentator observed, half the number of "determined and energetic" white men would complete more work more rapidly than would an African American crew. Tenancy additionally promised to convert Republican-dominated sugar parishes into politically dependable, white-populated districts. The idea of expelling African Americans from the plantation belt was not new; it dated to the mid-1850s, when Hinton Rowan Helper had proposed black colonization as a step toward formal separation of the races. Lincoln, too, had embraced such a position during the early years of the Civil War. With emancipation, however, local journalists rejected any sense of paternal oversight, urging white settlers to engage in a gritty race war. The labor market, one correspondent observed, was a prize fight where the freedman must "take his share of blows." If he can punch with "the power, energy, and skill of the Anglo-Saxon and Teutonic races," the former slave might remain; if not, he will be "counted out." Even if they could not deliver the knockout blow, white settlers promised to bring competition to the labor market, reduce wages, and bring the freedman to his "senses."[36]

The debate over tenancy continued unabated until the 1890s, but in the immediate aftermath of emancipation, white leasing ultimately foundered. Settlers, from within and outside the region, did not move to the sugar country in great numbers and, although local boosters crowed that "our people are becoming Yankeeized," the reality was less positive. Transplanted Northerners tended to join the landholding class, while smallholding settlers often converted cane fields into mixed crop farms producing tiny quantities of sugar. Clearly, such meager production could not provide the basis for long-term growth during Reconstruction.[37]

African American tenancy similarly failed. Not only did the division of labor (and the separation of the cultivation and production of cane sugar) implicit in small-farm tenancy contravene the logic of centralized plantations but planters also concluded that tenancy contributed to the scarcity of workers and the "labor famine" within the region. Black peasant production, moreover, proved racially problematic, as it implied the physical removal of the lessee from the plantation quarters. Behind these concerns, however, lay a deeper anxiety—namely the loss of control over the laboring classes inherent in tenancy. Only whites, planters assumed, were "economical and industrious" enough to be absented from the disciplined, rectilinear streets of workers' cottages. By contrast, only the drills of waged gang work and the watchful eye of the overseer, landlords deduced, would compel most African Americans to work. Similar anxieties made the share labor system problematic, too. As an alternative to monthly wages, some freedmen and white laborers received a share of the crop, usually between one-third and one-half, which they divided among themselves. For cash-strapped landlords, this arrangement had immediate utility as it deferred cash transactions until January, when the crop was sold. The advantages ended there. Indeed, most landlords came to agree that the "successful culture of sugar cane and the share system are incompatible and either one or the other must be abandoned." The share system ceded too much autonomy to the work crews, planters believed, and it dangerously exposed their economic dependency to the productivity of black workers.[38]

Despite their initial interest, neither tenancy nor shares offered an immediate solution to the labor problem. Both systems ceded too much autonomy to black workers in particular. Turning once again to the gang-based plantation system, landlords nevertheless faced a dire shortfall in labor. By 1869, only 10 percent of planters had a full complement of workers, and no more than three-eighths of the enslaved antebellum workforce continued in the fields. Women, in particular, absented themselves from work. Seeking a "new and harder" contract that might bring "system, organization, and the great law of all-order," planters longed to make labor "useful at all points of demand." This could be done, commentator Louis Bouchereau observed, by increasing the number and introducing a "new class of field laborers."[39]

Planters were intrigued by the prospect of recruiting foreign laborers, not solely as a workforce but as a means to strengthen their control over black workers. As Bouchereau optimistically noted, foreign competition would spark "a spirit of emulation" among African Americans. Others reflected more bluntly on the foreign labor movement. "The planters' backs are up and they mean business," one editor declared. "They are done petting negroes and paying two prices for half a day's work." Planters initially welcomed migrant workers and contracted them either for monthly wages (with half reserved until completion of the contract) or for a share of the crop. At the outset, immigrants appeared to resolve the labor problem. They worked well "and are perfectly manageable," Bouchereau declared about the newly arrived Germans. "With them an order is an order . . . with the negro an order is construed into an insult, however necessary to give." Dutch, Scandinavian, Italian, Portuguese, Irish, and French Canadians followed in turn, but despite the efforts of the state Bureau of Immigration (established in 1866), supply rarely matched demand. Confidence in foreign labor similarly turned sour when immigrants failed to match the landlords' expectations. Most particularly, the immigrants did not prove as tractable, or as slavish, as planters once had hoped. On Oakley Plantation, for instance, Swedish workers "slipped off" into New Orleans before they reached the estate, while those who continued on turned out drunk, demoralized, and idle. Portuguese workers likewise failed to make the grade—according to one planter, they labored slowly, inefficiently, and only when well fed. Another complained of the high costs incurred in recruiting immigrants, only to have them abandon the plantation midyear and go elsewhere for better wages. Italians similarly disappointed. Although Sicilians continued to labor in the cane fields well into the early twentieth century, most postbellum planters disparaged Italians as "a first class failure." Like the Portuguese and Swedes, the Italians proved a "noisy and worthless set" who brawled with the black cane hands, broke their contracts, and unsettled plantation affairs. Condemned by the same expectations that planters applied to freedpeople, landlords judged immigrants to be as inefficient and unreliable as those former slaves. As one plantation boss succinctly concluded, they "won't do."[40]

European immigrants were not alone in being tarnished by such proscriptive terms. As early as 1865, planters feverishly began to consider alternate labor supplies suitable for sugar work. Like their compatriots in tropical America and in the U.S. railroad industry, they alighted on the Chinese as a source of cheap and readily exploitable laborers. Chinese immigrants, planters hoped, would restore their fortunes and make planting "safe" again. By the early 1870s several hundred Chinese had arrived in the sugar district. At least initially, planters argued that Asians would "labor faithfully & satisfactorily" in the cane fields. Drawing analogies between the coolie trade and the slave trade, others optimistically hoped that Louisiana "will be far more prosperous than in the days of slavery" if "coolies" toiled within their midst. The elision of slavery and Chinese labor was no mistake. With labor agents in California, Memphis, and New Orleans ready to transport "the Pigtail" as a trafficked and racialized commodity, former slave lords enthusiastically welcomed the new and potentially tractable migrants. The fact that Chinese workers could be etymologically lumped together as racially defined coolies, just as planters utilized the umbrella term *negro* for all blacks irrespective of age, skill, or seniority, brought the two groups still closer together in the landlords' mind. Moreover, for those who yearned for the past, docile coolies appeared to toil with the muted hum planters associated with pastoral quietude. Although landlords evidently saw the phenotypical distinctions among Chinese and black laborers, the fact that most of the Chinese migrants were young, strong men fueled planter interest still more and conformed to their gender- and musculature-defined notions of the idealized sugar worker.[41]

As with the clamor for immigrant workers, planters hoped coolies would make labor "plentiful, [and] reduce wages." They also hoped that, when faced with Chinese competition, African Americans might become more pliable, "reliable," and "better workmen." But despite their early hopes, Chinese workers never quite solved the planters' labor problem. Better wages elsewhere lured immigrants away from the region, while those Chinese who went to Louisiana often proved unwilling converts to the sugar regime. They absconded from work, broke contracts, proved unsatisfactory in field labor, and were weak, inveterate gamblers, one journalist observed. Worse still, fighting between Asians, African Americans, and local whites destabilized plantation operations. By the mid-1870s, having been "tried to perfection," planters largely rejected Chinese labor. The problem lay in mistaken identities. As the *Louisiana Sugar Bowl* observed, the Chinaman appealed at first because he "was so much like the old Sambo and could be worked on the gang order." But appearances proved deceptive, for "he was not the man we took him for." Despite the costs, the stoppages, and the dependents that crowded the quarters, the "poor, starving...half-dead" migrant was no match for the African American who "had been at it his whole life." Ultimately discarding the racially marked figure of John Chinaman, planters concluded that "there is little prospect that John will trespass upon the claims of Sambo to any serious extent." In its failure, however, the experiment with Chinese workers reinforced the planters' commitment to black racialized labor. As one local editor observed, there "have been many *conspicuous successes* with free negroes, and *not a solitary one with any other*." Planters continued to experiment with migrant workers but, as each group failed in turn, landlords returned to the mantra of gang work and the centrality of African Americans to it.[42]

The problem as ever remained the availability and supply of black labor. To address this concern, landlords scoured the cotton belt for any spare hands. When this supply proved inadequate, planters renewed their longstanding interest in the labor of black Virginians. Indeed, in striking replication of antebellum precedent, where slave traders mined the Upper South to satiate the demand of the sugar elite, landlords hired recruitment agents to acquire Virginia hands. With a thousand Virginians required for the spring 1870 planting season, the *Planters' Banner* declared, "[Bayou] Teche will soon be Africanized again!" Yet, just as they ultimately abandoned foreign labor for failing to meet expectations, planters found that they could not replicate the volume or stability of the domestic slave trade. The cost of recruiting and transporting Virginians proved unworkable, former slaveholder Edward Gay discovered, because "they are so uncertain after you get them." Other planters combed neighboring states for laborers but, as with the East Coast trade, they quickly lost confidence in the recruitment process. Lots of "yeses," Robert Campbell Martin grumbled after a trip to east Texas, "but none that I have any confidence in." Like Martin, most landlords concluded that the instability, unreliability of, and high transportation costs incurred in the interregional labor trade were simply too great for most operators. Worse still, the cross-regional trade (upon which prewar sugar planters relied for slave laborers) now seemed in its postbellum guise to be as uncertain, unsafe, and fickle as the free workers it supplied.[43]

Renewing their interest in local and established black laborers, planters declared that the freedman, "especially on our alluvial lands, will never be supplanted." Others agreed, noting "it behoves us to make the best of the negro since he will probably be always a feature of our country." Redoubling their commitment to African American labor, plantation agriculture, gang work, and its racial corollary (white rule), landlords attempted to reassert their grip over land and labor. Indeed, with black women tending to withdraw from field work, planters reworked an old staple from the pro-slavery argument, namely that black males were "constitutionally" adapted to the production of sugar and that only "seasoned" hands from within the state could endure the rigors of Louisiana's semi-tropical climate and the sugar regime. As planters began to reimagine the ideal body for free labor sugar, women found themselves relegated to essential though nevertheless third-tier, gender-defined crews. Much as under slavery, muscle and an allegedly apt constitution for the travails of sugar defined the black male within the planters' racial conscience.[44]

"Thoroughly done for"

In re-racializing sugar as a definably black and male occupation, landlords considered it their right to regulate and control labor, irrespective of contract. "The planter who employs laborers of any kind, especially negroes," one agrarian warned his readers, "should be with them constantly enforcing and directing their work. The eye of the owner," he concluded, "is worth more than the labor of his hands." Robert Campbell Martin would have concurred. Like other native planters who had slavery "in the marrow of his bones," Martin resented the breakdown of authority on his estate. He disliked the erosion of traditional racial hierarchies and he longed for the physical power to enforce his command. When faced by a strike in November 1875, at the height of the harvest season, Martin docked wages and snarled, "I will not be trifled with, by white or black." Without the whip, planters lacked the coercive tools of slavery, but this did not appear to curtail Paul DeClouet's management style. When freedman Raphael challenged his employer, DeClouet used his fists in place of the lash, punching him to the ground. He quit that same day. Workers like Raphael may well have preferred to leave than face DeClouet's masterism, but the balance of power was far from equitably shared in this fight and countless others. As South Carolina secessionist turned postwar sugar planter William Porcher Miles discovered, planters still exercised the upper hand in labor relations. Describing a work stoppage, Miles's overseer bluntly observed: "The hands would not turn out yesterday... but I do not anticipate any trouble there or anywhere. Want of food will compel all hands to turn out soon. So I will just let them stew in their own juice until they are thoroughly done for." A year later, when faced with a walkout, Miles directed his overseer to enforce the pay rate or evict the workers within twenty-four hours. The following day, Miles intervened personally, ending the strike.[45]

Men of Martin and Miles' stamp wielded their authority with studied conviction. They understood that mastery necessitated highly personal forms of force and authority, and they believed that the "load of responsibility" rested upon the planter. Despite their wishful thinking, however, most landlords appreciated that commercial success rested on compromise and stability rather than conflict and authoritarianism. Besides, the Freedmen's Bureau (at least until the end of 1868, when it largely suspended field operations) could prosecute employers if they physically harassed their workers. As one overseer growled, "thar's no compellin' em. You can't hit a nigger now, but these d——d Yankee sons of b——s have you up and make you pay for it." Northern investors, moreover, who entered the sugar trade in the two decades following the Civil War contributed to the ideological shift toward contractualism and negotiation among planters. Instead of the "old time fellows" who cursed the Radicals, damned the Republicans, and condemned the African American to be "unreliable, untrustworthy, and unfit to be considered a human being," a new class of planter emerged. Although many of these émigrés ultimately became disillusioned with free labor, they entered the sugar trade without the ideological inheritance of slavery. As George Bovee observed, they considered farming a business and studied "the character of the labor they employ." Whether or not planters exhibited such rationalism, a growing body of postbellum landlords agreed that pro-slavery ideas now seemed completely redundant. Some of those who clung to the vestiges of legal bondage left the country and settled (often unsuccessfully) in pro-slavery Cuba and Brazil. In their place, however, came outside investors and the sons of antebellum planters. These investors, nevertheless, shared most of the racial and social assumptions of southern whites. They assumed white supremacy to be self-evident, and they quickly concurred that the planting and manufacturing of sugar necessitated gang labor and the maintenance of the plantation system.[46]

Navigating the uncertain terrain between controlling wage levels and the dangers of strike action nevertheless challenged old and new masters alike. As former slave lord Edward Gay recognized, this frequently required conciliation and strategic retreat on the part of employers. Planters accordingly acquiesced to demands for a dollar a day during the grinding season, and they reduced the proportion of the monthly wage that they withheld from one-half to one-third. Others responded to workplace pressure by paying cash wages in full at the end of each month. Across the industry, monthly wage rates rose above fifteen dollars by the mid-1870s. While some despaired and sold out, most planters attempted to compromise, though even here, they occasionally cloaked the language of labor relations with ante-bellum authoritarianism. Thus, when workers on Edward Gay's estate struck for seventy-five cents per day plus rations in October 1874, the veteran planter responded by advising his estate manager to "look squarely at the conditions . . . remove all feelings of hostility towards the hands and let the interest of the place be paramount." Gay had every reason to be concerned as neighboring planters clamored for labor and paid these rates. But for all his willingness to compromise, Gay was unwilling to forego his authority. Drawing upon decades of slave management, when advice leaflets urged masters to exercise their authority in a "mild, cool manner," Gay urged his manager to remain "calm and noncommittal" in pay disputes. As Gay concluded, this required a "sensible, shrewd, firm man" to visit his plantations and represent the landlord's interests. "Inattentive and incompetent" managers were unequal to the task at hand and, as Gay's associate Samuel Cranwill bluntly observed, "The effeminate and efete will have to give place to more competent and energetic men."[47]

Behind the robust, gender-charged language lay deeper anxieties. For all their personal interventions, Gay and Cranwill could not regulate free labor, and they remained perilously exposed to the dangers of collective action. In particular, the effect of wildcat strikes and sporadic unrest through the early 1870s combined with global competition to imperil the planter class. The expansion of European beet sugar, the heavy importation of Cuban sugar in the 1870s, the introduction of duty-free Hawaiian sugar in 1876, and the growth of cane farming in the Philippines and Java, moreover, provided new and unwelcome competition. Calls for federal appropriations to rebuild the decaying levee system fell on deaf ears, while popular derision at the sugar duty focused national ire on Louisiana producers once more. Such anxieties eroded confidence, as did the financial panic of 1873, which reduced money supplies nationwide. Cash-strapped planters responded by reducing monthly wages and turning to the state to protect their economic interests. These lessons came into relief in January 1874, when cane workers in Terrebonne Parish responded to a wage cut with mass strike action. Demanding monthly wages of twenty dollars, more than two hundred cane workers gathered at the Zion Church near Houma to call for strike action. Violent confrontations broke out, notably on Henry Minor's Southdown Plantation. Telegraphing Governor William Pitt Kellogg's office, Minor requested state militia to disband "the Negro riot," as whites euphemistically termed it. The following day, January 14, the New Orleans Metropolitan Police arrived in Houma, followed by troops under the command of former Confederate General James Longstreet. Although the strike ended in stalemate, the unrest demonstrated that, when faced by a phalanx of state and planter authority, labor unrest could be quelled. If a Republican governor (a Vermont carpetbagger, no less) could be persuaded to dispatch troops, conservatives eagerly anticipated the restoration of sympathetic white Democrats who might ally state and planter interests still further.[48]

Fusing grass-roots militarization with white-line voter mobilization, conservatives aimed to replace Republican with Democratic administrations at parish and gubernatorial levels. The counter-revolution extended to the countryside, where the labor problem was met head on. As George W. Stafford reported to the *Louisiana Democrat*, "In a war of the races . . . there can be *no quarter*." He did not mince words. At Colfax, on the northern margins of the state's sugar-producing belt, white paramilitaries killed more than one hundred black Republicans in April 1873. By the spring of the following year, white anxieties reached fever pitch as African Americans began mustering militia units in the aftermath of the Terrebonne strike. The presence of militarized Republicans predictably alarmed local whites, who called for a counter-thrust. Like many of his class, Paul DeClouet joined a White League and went on night patrol with fellow white supremacists to overturn the black challenge. For recalcitrant men like DeClouet, the White League promised violent salvation and redemption from "the burning shame and approbation of an Africanised and disgraced country."[49]

In April 1874, the Mississippi River burst its banks. More than twelve thousand square miles in Louisiana lay submerged in the worst flood on record. Like the dark water that spilled through gaps in the dilapidated levees, white Louisianans attempted to stem the African American challenge. The ten thousand strong White Leagues could not turn the flood waters back but, emboldened by the Colfax massacre, paramilitaries abandoned any illusion of secrecy. Harrying black and white Republican officeholders across the state, the league seized local political power and challenged Republicans from the grass roots up. By midsummer, they turned from local to statewide politics. On September 14, more than eight thousand armed whites, most of whom were Confederate veterans, launched a coup d'etat on the streets of New Orleans and captured City Hall. It was a dramatic and audacious claim for white home rule. Only the intervention of President Grant and the use of federal troops prevented a rout. Governor Kellogg remained in office following the debacle, but his authority drained away as the forces of political, racial, and landed conservatism cohered behind the movement for white Democratic rule.[50]

The centennial elections of 1876 proved to be as fraught as the political climate. Sugar planter and Democrat Francis T. Nicholls claimed the governorship, as did his Republican rival. Their fate, however, lay in Washington, where the presidential election lay deadlocked, with the disputed votes in Louisiana, South Carolina, and Florida. In return for those votes and the election of Rutherford B. Hayes, the Republicans promised to recognize Democratic control of the South and avoid intervening in local affairs. In Louisiana, the remaining federal troops withdrew and Nicholls assumed the governor's office. The election of Hayes and Nicholls ended fifteen years of Reconstruction in Louisiana. This was among the longest and most protracted readjustment of any southern state in the Union, but as black Louisianan Henry Adams acutely observed, his state—like the rest of South—now lay in "the hands of the very men that held us as slaves."[51]

On the land, planters similarly attempted to disempower African Americans in the name of white redemption. Lobbying for collective action, first as an agricultural grange, though more concretely as the Louisiana Sugar Planters Association (LSPA), employers attempted to secure collectively what eluded them privately: authority and control over the cane hands. Founded in 1877, the LSPA fused old and new masters in one organization. Veteran slaveholder Duncan Kenner (author of the black codes) served as chairman, with Ohio Democrat John Dymond as vice president. Under their leadership, the LSPA sought to address the challenges posed by the international market and the vagaries of Louisiana labor. The LSPA lobbied for protective tariffs and urged Congress to fund the levee system. It also promoted scientific farming, attempted to regulate the market, and tried to assure more stable commodity prices. But it was in labor relations that the LSPA had its most significant short-term impact. The organization curtailed the physical mobility of cane hands, it reduced wages and halted the payment of monthly wages in full, and it reverted to withholding one-third of the cash payment until the close of harvest. This triggered considerable bickering, but after fifteen years of waged labor in the cane fields, planters wielded their newly acquired political and collective clout. As one landlord crowed, "Labor will go to the wall and ultimately bear the brunt of injuries."[52]

For many planters, the LSPA and Democratic rule offered a state-sanctioned solution to the labor problem and the problem of freedom. But redemption incorporated more than just politics; indeed, it promised to rein in free labor and convert the wayward cane hand into a dependent and profitable employee. Planters hoped that, once fully redeemed and purged of his insubordinate Republican ways, the "disciplined labor of the American negro" might restore fortunes and allow Louisiana's cane growers to flourish again. In their minds, like those of their slaveholding predecessors, discipline, regulation, and mastery rested at the core of business success. Turning to the state as a guarantor of their power and authority, planters envisioned a future where the state sustained the plantation mode and regulated labor. They did not have to wait long for such a collusion of military, civic, and private authority. In 1878 Nicholls's administration founded Louisiana's National Guard. Manned by White League veterans, the National Guard provided state authorities with a reliable military force to sustain white-line government and the interests of landed capital. The following year, the redrafted state constitution reduced property taxes to paltry levels and considerably strengthened gubernatorial power at the expense of the more populist state legislature. The federal government also assumed command of flood control on the Mississippi and provided funding for levee construction.[53]

By 1880, African Americans faced a powerful amalgamation of interests. Over the past decade, they had watched the planters regroup and had endured paramilitary terror at the ballot box. Some left for Kansas and the hope of securing landed independence. The vast majority, however, remained on the land and attempted to better their conditions by striking and through labor unrest. For fifteen years, these tools had served the black community well. When cane workers struck in April 1880, however, demanding "a dollar a day or Kansas," armed troops quelled the unrest. Planters were shaken, but with the National Guard deployed to uphold planter authority, estate managers exercised considerable leverage in labor negotiations. Although frequent use of armed troops undermined their individual authority as land and labor lords, the collusion of state authority and planter dominion acutely affected the black community and its long-term capacity to organize in the sugar fields.[54]

Over the next decade, cane workers continued to mobilize but, bound to wage labor and to the regulated order of sugar production, these workers encountered only the narrowest and most fragmentary of freedoms. Trapped within a regime rooted—historically, culturally, and materially—in the language and ideology of mastery, Louisiana's cane workers found themselves mired in dependency and with state-sanctioned limits to free labor. These factors alone gravely impeded the workers' capacity to shape plantation labor and define their own freedom, autonomy, and independence. For their part, Louisiana's sugar planting elite clung tenaciously to the concept of regulated, deferential labor, to the maintenance of the plantation system, and to their racial and class power. Although contract replaced the highly intrusive and personal forms of racial power (encoded in slavery), these legacies of enslavement endured through Reconstruction and beyond. Successive generations of planters grumbled about the "labor problem" but, with their power bolstered by the state, the sugar elite grimly addressed the "problem of freedom too." They restricted the economic and political liberties of free labor, and within their minds—if not always in reality—they converted unruly cane hands into black dependent labor. When workers struck again in 1887, planters responded characteristically and with predictable results; this time thirty cane workers lay dead. As planter Mary Pugh recorded in stark racial clarity, the Thibodaux massacre resolved the depressing question: "Who is to rule, the nigger or the White man? For the next 50 years." Pugh's conclusions proved all too prophetic as Louisiana—like the rest of the American South—descended into the racial abyss of Jim Crow.[55]

Conclusion

❧

TWENTY YEARS AFTER Lincoln signed the Emancipation Proclamation, Frederick Douglass addressed a mass meeting in Washington. The topic had vexed him for most of his life—the enduring effect of slavery and the problem of freedom. Responding to the Supreme Court ruling (*United States v. Stanley*) that undermined the constitutional protections of the Fourteenth Amendment and struck down the Civil Rights Act (1875), Douglass declared that "we have been, as a class, grievously wounded, wounded in the house of our friends." As the veteran abolitionist announced, the Court's decision "has humbled the Nation" and made liberty "weak." "The whole essence of the thing," Douglass avowed, "is a studied purpose to degrade and stamp out the liberties of a race. It is the old spirit of slavery, and nothing else." African American leaders across the country affirmed Douglass's damning indictment of the "national deterioration" in race relations and his belief that the spirit or power of slavery lingered within the American political and racial conscience.[1]

Douglass's frustration derived from the broken promises of Reconstruction. Former slave Henry Adams understood this from personal experience. Born a slave in Georgia, Adams was transported to Louisiana in the 1850s. There, he and his family labored on cotton plantations in northeastern Louisiana. Having been hired out under slavery, Adams acquired a little property and a relatively forthright demeanor. In the aftermath of emancipation, Adams took to the roads before joining the U.S. Army, where he learned to read and write. He rose through the ranks and served in federal units across Louisiana. Appalled by the chicanery of white Democrats and the violence inflicted on his race, Adams organized a secret committee to gather information on the condition of African Americans in the rural parishes and to promote grass-roots political activism. Voting for the first time in 1870, Adams swiftly gained the attention of local whites, who threatened to kill him for encouraging black voting and "spoil[ing] the other negroes." When faced by the insurgent racism and political intimidation of Louisiana's White Leagues, Adams began to consider emigrating. Believing that it was "utterly impossible to live with the whites of Louisiana," Adams and a group of fellow "laboring men" helped form a local Colonization Council in 1874 to "better our condition." That September, the Colonization Council lobbied President Ulysses S. Grant, requesting their removal to Liberia. Three years later, they wrote to President Rutherford B. Hayes, declaring that, twelve years after emancipation, black southerners could no longer live in "peace, harmony, and happiness." With their constitutional rights willfully ignored, exodus and colonization in Africa offered the "only hope," Adams argued, for African Americans.[2]

As Frederick Douglass and Henry Adams affirmed, black freedom was not easily attained nor was it readily surrendered by white Americans. Both black leaders recognized the erosive power of slaveholding and the "accustomed channels," Douglass observed, of racial prejudice. Adams, in particular, pointedly asked: "Could [we] stay under a people who had held us under bondage or not?" The combative African Methodist Episcopal (AME) missionary Henry McNeal Turner answered in the negative, declaring in 1906 that "hell is an improvement on the United States where the Negro is concerned." As Reverend William Henry Coston lamented, Republicans and Democrats alike were culpable for the broken promises of Reconstruction. "We have nothing to gain from either party," he told fellow African Americans. "One has betrayed us, the other murders us with impunity."

This book has placed the anger and despair of these black leaders in context and examined the legacies of slavery and the limits to both freedom and free will for African Americans in the mid-nineteenth century. It has done so on three interlocking levels, which descend from the conceptual approaches we adopt in studying African American history, to the ideological limits to presidential emancipation, to the grass roots where former slaves and enslavers contested the terms of free labor and the nature of freedom in the postwar years. The three essays underscore the limits and material determinants of agency, the incremental and racially conservative nature of slave emancipation, and the enduring relevance of slavery and the particular organization of production and dominion to the postwar settlement.[3]

In conclusion, this book does not "readjust the sliding switch away from 'agency' and toward 'power' or away from the oppressed and toward the oppressors," as Walter Johnson indicates, but it offers some interpretive ways to consider the power, determinants, and discourse that shaped and defined the history of black freedom in the era of slavery and emancipation.

NOTES

Introduction

1. Frederick Douglass, *My Bondage and My Freedom* (New York: Miller, Orton & Mulligan, 1855), 273, 246–247; "The Day of Jubilee Comes: An Address delivered in Rochester, New York, on 28 December 1862," in *The Frederick Douglass Papers*, ed. John W. Blassingame, *Series One: Speeches, Debates, and Interviews*, vol. 3, *1855–63* (New Haven: Yale University Press, 1985), 545; David W. Blight, *Frederick Douglass' Civil War: Keeping Faith in Jubilee* (Baton Rouge: Louisiana State University Press, 1989), 14.

2. W. E. B. Du Bois, *Black Reconstruction in America, 1860–1880* (New York: Free Press, 1998 [1935]), 55; Steven Hahn, *The Political Worlds of Slavery and Freedom* (Cambridge: Harvard University Press, 2009), 55; Steven Hahn, Steven F. Miller, Susan E. O'Donovan, John C. Rodrigue, and Leslie S. Rowland, *Freedom: A Documentary History of Emancipation, 1861–1867, Series 3*, vol. 1, *Land and Labor, 1865* (Chapel Hill: University of North Carolina Press, 2008), 1–70.

3. Blight, *Douglass' Civil War*, 191; James M. McPherson, *Abraham Lincoln and the Second American Revolution* (New York: Oxford University Press, 1991), 6.

4. The key work on Reconstruction remains Eric Foner, *Reconstruction: America's Unfinished Revolution, 1863–1877* (New York: Harper & Row, 1988). More recently, consult Michael W. Fitzgerald, *Splendid Failure: Postwar Reconstruction in the American South* (Chicago: Ivan R. Dee, 2007).

5. Blight, *Douglass' Civil War*, 217, 221; Stephen Cresswell, *Rednecks, Redeemers, and Race: Mississippi after Reconstruction, 1877–1917* (Jackson: University Press of Mississippi, 2006), 55.

6. Peter A. Coclanis, "The Captivity of a Generation," *William and Mary Quarterly* 61 (July 2004): 544–555; John C. Rodrigue, "Black Agency after Slavery,"

in *Reconstructions: New Perspectives on the Postbellum United States*, ed. Thomas J. Brown (New York: Oxford University Press, 2006), 41.

7. Blight, *Douglass' Civil War*, 208–209.

Agency: A Ghost Story

1. Karl Marx, *The Eighteenth Brumaire of Louis Bonaparte* (New York: International, 1963), 15. Born in New York City in 1928 to Jewish immigrant parents, Gutman grew up within a liberal, left-leaning family. He flirted with communism and campaigned in 1948 for the Progressive Party presidential candidate Henry Wallace (who sought to end racial segregation, extend voting rights to all African Americans, and grant universal health care). Having studied at Columbia for his masters degree, when he wrote about labor's demands for public works during the depression years of the 1870s, Gutman subsequently enrolled at the University of Wisconsin, where he worked on the history of American labor during the Panic of 1873. Madison, during the years when Gutman was there, was home to some of the nation's foremost historians of labor and class, and it was in this environment that Gutman honed his intellectual agenda and his commitment to writing a "new" social history of the American working class. After teaching in New Jersey during the tumultuous early years of the civil rights movement, Gutman joined the faculty at the State University of New York, Buffalo, in 1963.

2. E. P. Thompson, *The Making of the English Working Class* (New York: Vintage Books, 1964), 10. For the debates about Marxism and history in which Thompson was engaged, see Geoff Eley, *A Crooked Line: From Cultural History to the History of Society* (Ann Arbor: University of Michigan Press, 2005), 48–59.

3. Thompson, *Making of the English Working Class*, 9–10.

4. "Interview with Herbert Gutman," in Herbert G. Gutman, *Power and Culture: Essays on the History of the American Working Class*, ed. Ira Berlin (New York: Pantheon Books, 1987), 342–343; Herbert Gutman, "The Workers' Search for Power: Labor in the Gilded Age," in Gutman, *Power and Culture*, 70, 91. For Gutman's later comment on Marxism, see "Interview with Herbert Gutman," 342–344; Herbert Gutman, "Work, Culture, and Society in Industrializing America, 1815–1919," in Herbert G. Gutman, *Work, Culture, and Society in Industrializing America* (New York: Vintage Books, 1977), 5–7, 13–19, 39, 55. The essay was originally published in the *American Historical Review* 78 (1973): 531–588.

5. Gutman, "Work, Culture, and Society," 71, 22–23. See also "Interview with Herbert Gutman," 337–339.

6. Gutman, "Work, Culture, and Society," 67–74. See also "Interview with Herbert Gutman," 346 ("the central value of historical understanding is to transform

historical givens into contingencies") and Gutman, "Historical Consciousness in Contemporary America," in Gutman, *Power and Culture*, 395–412.

7. Gutman, "Work, Culture, and Society," 27, 46, 65, 74–75.

8. Toni Morrison, *Playing in the Dark: Whiteness and the Literary Imagination* (Cambridge: Harvard University Press, 1992), 6. See also Avery Gordon, *Ghostly Matters: Haunting and the Sociological Imagination* (Minneapolis: University of Minnesota Press, 1997); Gutman, "Work, Culture, and Society," 12–13, 58–59n41.

9. Gutman, *Work, Culture, and Society*, xiii–xiv. Interestingly, Gutman had used the exact same joke to close the preface he wrote for Sterling D. Spero and Abram L. Harris, eds., *The Black Worker: The Negro in the Labor Movement* (New York: Atheneum, 1968), xiii; Mary White Ovington, "The Negro in the Trades Unions of New York," *Annals of the American Academy of Political and Social Science* 27 (May 1906): 96.

10. Gutman, "Work, Culture, and Society," 16–17n14, 58–59n41, 74. As dissonant as this passage seems today, one must pause and remember that for Gutman the term *preindustrial* was a form of high praise. Having paused and remembered that, one might then move on to see his usage as a demonstration of the larger point of this essay (stop reading here and return to the text if you're enjoying the suspense): Gutman was stretching the terms of his analysis to the point that they ruptured into dis-synthesis. The given set of terms surrounding African Americans in the modern world simply did not allow for a valorizing resignification of the idea of blacks as temporally delayed and developmentally static (in the way that the set of terms surrounding "immigration," at least in the case of Europeans, arguably did).

11. Gutman, "Work, Culture, and Society," 67–68.

12. Thompson, *Making of the English Working Class*, 12. "Nor was it [the shift to the focus on "slave belief and behavior"] simply a response to the civil rights and black power movements. In these same years, historians studying subordinate classes other than Afro-Americans grew increasingly dissatisfied with the prevailing reactive models used to explain their belief and behavior." Herbert Gutman, "The Black Family in Slavery and Freedom: A Revised Perspective," in Gutman, *Power and Culture*, 357.

13. Ira Berlin, "Herbert G. Gutman and the American Working Class," in Gutman, *Power and Culture*, 25–31; Herbert Gutman, "Peter H. Clark: Pioneer Socialist, 1877," *Journal of Negro Education* 34, no. 4 (Autumn 1965): 413–418; "Preface," in Sterling D. Spero and Abram L. Harris, eds., *The Black Worker: The Negro in the Labor Movement* (New York: Atheneum, 1968), vii–xiii; "The Negro and the United Mine Workers of America: The Career and Letters of Richard L. Davis and Something of Their Meaning, 1890–1900," originally published in Julius

Jacobson, ed., *The Negro and the American Labor Movement* (New York, 1968), 49–127, reprinted in Herbert Gutman, ed., *Work, Culture, and Society*, 121–208; "Labor in the Land of Lincoln," in Gutman, *Power and Culture*, 117–212. The last of these was written in these years but remained unpublished until after Gutman's death in 1985.

14. Gutman, "The Negro and the United Mine Workers," 121–208, esp. 194 (and n110), 195, 204–208. Gutman's account of Davis, the UMW, and "inter-racialism" generally was debunked by Herbert Hill in "Myth-Making as Labor History: Herbert Gutman and the United Mine Workers of America," *International Journal of Politics, Culture, and Society* 2, no. 2 (Winter 1988): 132–200. For this ongoing and critical discussion (as well as some discussion of "race and class" beyond the history [or not] of "inter-racial" labor solidarity), see Nell Irvin Painter, *The Narrative of Hosea Hudson: The Life and Times of a Black Radical*, originally published 1979 (New York: W. W. Norton, 1994); William H. Harris, *The Harder We Run: Black Workers since the Civil War* (New York: Oxford University Press, 1982); Elsa Barkley Brown, "Womanist Consciousness: Maggie Lena Walker and the Independent Order of Saint Luke," *Signs* 14 (1989): 610–633; Barbara Jeanne Fields, "Slavery, Race, and Ideology in the United States of America," *New Left Review* 181 (May–June 1990): 95–118; Robin D. G. Kelley, *Hammer and Hoe: Alabama Communists during the Great Depression* (Chapel Hill: University of North Carolina Press, 1990); David R. Roediger, *The Wages of Whiteness: Race and the Making of the American Working Class* (New York: Verso, 1990); Tera W. Hunter, *To 'Joy My Freedom: Southern Black Women's Lives and Labors after the Civil War* (Cambridge: Harvard University Press, 1997); Eric Arnesen, *Waterfront Workers of New Orleans: Race, Class, and Politics, 1863–1923* (New York: Oxford University Press, 1991), *Brotherhoods of Color: Black Railroad Workers and the Struggle for Equality* (Cambridge: Harvard University Press, 2001), and "Whiteness and the Historians' Imagination," *International Labor and Working-Class History* 60 (2001): 3–32; Michael K. Honey, *Going Down Jericho Road: The Memphis Strike, Martin Luther King's Last Campaign* (New York: W. W. Norton, 2007).

15. Herbert G. Gutman, *The Black Family in Slavery and Freedom, 1750–1925* (New York: Pantheon Books, 1976), xviii; Ira Berlin, "Herbert G. Gutman and the American Working Class," in Gutman, *Power and Culture*, 41–44; Stanley M. Elkins, *Slavery: A Problem in American Institutional and Intellectual Life*, 3rd ed. (Chicago: University of Chicago Press, 1976), 88–89.

16. Office of Policy Planning and Research, U.S. Department of Labor, *The Negro Family: The Case for National Action* (March 1965), www.dol.gov/oasam/programs/history/webid-moynihan.htm. Moynihan was not alone; E. Franklin Frazier described the slave family as fatherless or mother-centered, in *The Negro Family in the United States* (Chicago: University of Chicago Press, 1939).

17. See also Gutman, "Black Family: A Revised Perspective," esp. 359–370. Gutman's essentially liberal and comparative strategy for vindicating the history of African Americans had precedent. As early as 1952, historian Kenneth Stampp had called for a "completely objective study" of slavery without any preestablished assumptions of racial inferiority. His 1956 study *The Peculiar Institution* embodied this perspective. It began with a clear statement that guided his approach: "The slaves were merely ordinary human beings, that innately Negroes *are*, after all, only white men with black skins, nothing more, nothing less." Or, conversely, "It would serve my purpose as well," Stampp continued, "to call Caucasians black men with white skins." In other words, he seemed just like anyone else. During the era of black power and cultural nationalism, scholars challenged Stampp's race-blind liberalism, particularly its enabling assertion that slaves were "culturally rootless people." Kenneth M. Stampp, *The Peculiar Institution: Slavery in the Antebellum South* (New York: Vintage, 1956), vii–ix, 364; John W. Blassingame, *The Slave Community: Plantation Life in the Ante-bellum South* [originally published 1972], rev. ed. (New York: Oxford University Press, 1979); Lawrence W. Levine, *Black Culture and Black Consciousness: Afro-American Folk Thought from Slavery to Freedom* (New York: Oxford University Press, 1977); Sterling Stuckey, *Slave Culture: Nationalist Thought and the Foundations of Black America* (New York: Oxford University Press, 1987).

18. Eugene D. Genovese, *Roll, Jordan, Roll: The World the Slaves Made* (New York: Vintage, 1972), 71–75.

19. Ibid., 598, 659. The following paragraphs are based upon my twenty-fifth anniversary review of *Roll, Jordan, Roll*, "A Nettlesome Classic Turns Twenty-Five," *Common-Place* 1, no. 4 (July 2001), www.common-place.org.

20. Elizabeth Fox-Genovese and Eugene D. Genovese, "The Political Crisis of Social History: A Marxian Perspective," *Journal of Social History* 10 (Autumn 1976): 205, 214, 212, 219, 213, 215.

21. Gutman, *Black Family in Slavery and Freedom*, 32, 311 (see also 316); Fox-Genovese and Genovese, "Political Crisis of Social History," 207.

22. Gutman, "Black Family: A Revised Perspective," 364.

23. Fox-Genovese and Genovese, "Political Crisis of Social History," 213.

24. Herbert G. Gutman, "Labor History and the 'Sartre Question,'" in Gutman, *Power and Culture*, 326. For Gutman's vision of "a general social history of the American people," see "Interview with Herbert Gutman," 348 (likewise 335).

25. "Interview with Herbert Gutman," 346; Gutman, "Black Family: A Revised Perspective," 358.

26. American Social History Project, *Who Built America? Working People and the Nation's Economy, Politics, Culture, and Society* (New York: Pantheon Books, 1992), x–xi.

27. I am using the term *cultural dominant* in the way suggested by Raymond Williams in *Marxism and Literature* (New York: Oxford University Press, 1977), 121–128.

28. "Interview with Herbert Gutman," 346.

29. Nell Irvin Painter, "Southern History across the Color Line," in her *Southern History across the Color Line* (Chapel Hill: University of North Carolina Press, 2002), 1–14 (including a paean to Herbert Gutman on 5–6); Sterling Stuckey, *Slave Culture: Nationalist Thought and the Foundations of Black America* (New York: Oxford University Press, 1987); Lawrence W. Levine, *Black Culture and Black Consciousness: Afro-American Folk Thought from Slavery to Freedom* (New York: Oxford University Press, 1977); Michael Angleo Gomez, *Exchanging Our Country Marks: The Transformation of African Identities in the Colonial and Antebellum South* (Chapel Hill: University of North Carolina Press, 1998); Nikhil Pal Singh, *Black Is a Country: Race and the Unfinished Struggle for Democracy* (Cambridge: Harvard University Press, 2004); Sidney Mintz and Richard Price, *The Birth of African-American Culture: An Anthropological Perspective* (Boston: Beacon Press, 1992); Ira Berlin, *Many Thousands Gone: The First Two Centuries of Slavery in North America* (Cambridge: Harvard University Press, 1998); Vincent Brown, *The Reaper's Garden: Death and Power in the World of Atlantic Slavery* (Cambridge: Harvard University Press, 2007); Stephanie Smallwood, *Saltwater Slavery: A Middle Passage from Africa to American Diaspora* (Cambridge: Harvard University Press, 2007); Herbert Aptheker, *American Negro Slave Revolts* (New York: International Publishers, 1963); Robin D. G. Kelley, *Race Rebels: Culture, Politics, and the Black Working Class* (New York: Free Press, 1994); David R. Roediger, *The Wages of Whiteness: Race and the Making of the American Working Class* (London: Verso, 1991); Peter Linebaugh and Marcus Rediker, *The Many-Headed Hydra: Sailors, Slaves, Commoners, and the Hidden History of the Revolutionary Atlantic* (Boston: Beacon, 2000); Adam Green, *Selling the Race: Culture, Community, and Black Chicago, 1940–1955* (Chicago: University of Chicago Press, 2007); Darlene Clark Hine, *Hine Sight: Black Women and the Reconstruction of American History* (Brooklyn: Carlson Publishing, 1994); Nell Irvin Painter, *Sojourner Truth: A Life, A Symbol* (New York: W. W. Norton, 1996); Deborah Gray White, *Ar'n't I a Woman? Female Slaves in the Plantation South* (New York: W. W. Norton, 1985); Tera Hunter, *To 'Joy my Freedom: Southern Black Women's Lives and Labors after the Civil War* (Cambridge: Harvard University Press, 1997); Jennifer Morgan, *Laboring Women: Reproduction and Gender in New World Slavery* (Philadelphia: University of Pennsylvania Press, 2004).

30. For the sort of process I am describing, in which alternative and oppositional sets of terms are contained, though never fully and never finally, within a hegemonic set of terms, see Williams, *Marxism and Literature*, 107–127, esp. 114.

31. Philip D. Morgan, *Slave Counterpoint: Black Culture in the Eighteenth-Century Chesapeake and Lowcountry* (Chapel Hill: University of North Carolina Press, 1998), xxii. Morgan's usage is especially interesting for framing a book that self-consciously attempts to resist the "romanticized" terms of histories of slavery written from "the bottom up" (see xxiv); evidence, I would suggest, of the extent to which the "agency" discussion magnetizes even efforts to escape its conventions. Speaking of twice-told tales, see Walter Johnson, "On Agency," *Journal of Social History* 37 (Fall 2003): 113–124; "Freedom's Servant: Slavery, Freedom, and Reparations as a Theory of History," *Raritan* (Fall 2007).

32. See William H. Sewell Jr., *Logics of History: Social Theory and Social Transformation* (Chicago: University of Chicago Press, 2005). On the question of "determination," see also Williams, *Marxism and Literature*, esp. 75–89, 145–212; Louis Althusser, "Contradiction and Overdetermination," in his *For Marx* (London: Verso, 2005), 87–128.

33. Karl Marx, "On the Jewish Question," www.marxists.org/archive/marx/works/1844/jewish-question/. For the development of the question of historical subjectivity into an engagement with and critique of Marxism itself, see Cedric J. Robinson, *Black Marxism: The Making of the Black Radical Tradition*, 2nd ed. (Chapel Hill: University of North Carolina Press, 2000); Lisa Lowe, *Immigrant Acts: On Asian American Cultural Politics* (Durham: Duke University Press, 1996); Dipesh Chakrabarty, *Provincializing Europe: Postcolonial Thought and Historical Difference* (Princeton: Princeton University Press, 2000); and Singh, *Black Is a Country*. In addition to the politico-liberalism that immanently formats its version of historical time, it might be argued that the new social history's version of spaces was concomitantly formatted by the parameters of the nation-state. Gutman's work and the "new social history" in general are characterized by a sort of pointillist nationalism in which American history might eventually be composed of its various physically bounded community studies. Gutman's quest for a general theory of labor history was immanently structured by his desire to reclaim the term *America* for its immigrants and its working people. And yet, in spite of this noble premise, it unfolded in seemingly willful ignorance of the spatially dynamic and imperial aspect of American economic development: of the Louisiana Purchase, the War of 1812, Indian Removal, the Mexican-American War, the Spanish-American War, the Vietnam War, the work of William Appleman Williams, etc. The present turn toward transnational approaches to American history reflects a general sense of the exhaustion of framing parameters of social history.

34. Johnson, "On Agency," 115; Walter Johnson, "White Lies: Human Property and Domestic Slavery aboard the Slave Ship *Creole*," *Atlantic Studies* 5 (August 2008): 256–258; Martin R. Delany, *Blake or the Huts of America*, ed. Floyd J. Miller, originally published 1861–62 (Boston: Beacon Press, 1970), 40. Exemplary of

renewed emphasis on material life in this historiography of slavery are: on repro-duction, Morgan, *Laboring Women*, and Marie Jenkins Schwartz, *Birthing a Slave: Motherhood and Medicine in the Antebellum South* (Cambridge: Harvard University Press, 2006); on the landscape and material space, Stephanie M. H. Camp, *Closer to Freedom: Enslaved Women and Everyday Resistance in the Plantation South* (Chapel Hill: University of North Carolina Press, 2004), and Anthony E. Kaye, *Joining Places: Slave Neighborhoods in the Old South* (Chapel Hill: University of North Caro-lina Press, 2007); on labor, Richard Follett, *The Sugar Masters: Planters and Slaves in Louisiana's Cane World, 1820–1860* (Baton Rouge: Louisiana State University Press, 2005), and Susan Eva O'Donovan, *Becoming Free in the Cotton South* (Cam-bridge: Harvard University Press, 2007); and, on death, Brown, *Reaper's Garden*.

35. Marx, "On the Jewish Question"; Supreme Court of the United States, No. 05-908, *Parents Involved in Community Schools v. Seattle School District No. 1, et al.*, www.law.cornell.edu/supct/html/05-908.ZS.html.

Abraham Lincoln, Colonization, and the Rights of Black Americans

1. Ted Widmer, ed., *American Speeches* (New York: Library of America, 2006), 2:80.

2. T. Harry Williams, *Lincoln and the Radicals* (Madison: University of Wiscon-sin Press, 1941); William B. Hesseltine, *Lincoln and the War Governors* (New York: Alfred A. Knopf, 1948); Benjamin Quarles, *Lincoln and the Negro* (New York: Ox-ford University Press, 1962).

3. Eric Foner, *The Fiery Trial: Abraham Lincoln and American Slavery* (New York: W. W. Norton, 2010).

4. Douglas L. Wilson and Rodney O. Davis., eds., *Herndon's Informants* (Ur-bana: University of Illinois Press, 1998), 13, 61; David Davis to Abraham Lincoln, August 3, 1858, Abraham Lincoln Papers, Library of Congress; J. McCan Davis, *Abraham Lincoln: His Book* (New York: Philips McClure, 1903).

5. Roy P. Basler, ed., *Collected Works of Abraham Lincoln*, 9 vols. (New Bruns-wick: Rutgers University Press, 1953–55), 2:255; 3:327–328.

6. Ibid., 5:534–535; Albert Mordell, ed., *Civil War and Reconstruction: Selected Essays by Gideon Welles* (New York: Twayne Publishers, 1959), 250; Lerone Ben-nett, *Forced into Glory: Abraham Lincoln's White Dream* (Chicago: Johnson Pub-lishing Co., 2000); Don E. Fehrenbacher, "Only His Stepchildren: Lincoln and the Negro," *Civil War History* 20 (December 1974): 307. In William Lee Miller's study of Lincoln's moral leadership, *Lincoln's Virtues: An Ethical Biography* (New York: Alfred A. Knopf, 2002), 354, colonization receives a brief mention three-quarters of the way through the book. In her 800-page work on Lincoln and his cabinet, *Team of Rivals: The Political Genius of Abraham Lincoln* (New York: Simon

& Schuster, 2005), Doris Kearns Goodwin says almost nothing about colonization. Michael Lind, *What Lincoln Believed: The Values and Convictions of America's Greatest President* (New York: Doubleday, 2005), follows Bennett in stressing Lincoln's commitment to colonization.

7. *Harper's Weekly*, April 5, 1862; Eric Foner, *Nothing but Freedom: Emancipation and Its Legacy* (Baton Rouge: Louisiana State University Press, 1983), 8–23. For decades, the only full-length book on colonization was P. J. Staudenraus, *The African Colonization Movement, 1816–1865* (New York: Columbia University Press, 1961). But several important works have appeared of late, notably Eric Burin, *Slavery and the Peculiar Solution: A History of the American Colonization Society* (Gainesville: University of Florida Press, 2005), and Claude A. Clegg III, *The Price of Liberty: African Americans and the Making of Liberia* (Chapel Hill: University of North Carolina Press, 2004). An important contribution to the renewed interest in colonization was David Brion Davis, "Reconsidering the Colonization Movement: Leonard Bacon and the Problem of Evil," *Intellectual History Newsletter* 14 (1992): 3–16.

8. Thomas Jefferson, *Notes on the State of Virginia* (Philadelphia: Prichard & Hall, 1788), 154, 199–202; Merrill D. Peterson, ed., *Thomas Jefferson: Writings* (New York: Library of America, 1984), 1484–1487.

9. Isaac V. Brown, *Biography of the Rev. Robert Finley*, 2nd ed. (Philadelphia, 1857), 103–115; Paul Goodman, *Of One Blood: Abolitionism and the Origins of Racial Equality* (Berkeley: University of California Press, 1998), 14–18; Douglas R. Egerton, "Averting a Crisis: The Proslavery Critique of the American Colonization Society," *Civil War History* 43 (June 1997): 147; Daniel W. Howe, *The Political Culture of the American Whigs* (Chicago: University of Chicago Press, 1984), 136; Robert V. Remini, *Henry Clay: Statesman for the Union* (New York: W. W. Norton, 1991), 491–492, 508; James F. Hopkins, ed., *Papers of Henry Clay*, 10 vols. (Lexington: University of Kentucky Press, 1959–91), 8:812; 10:372–376; Basler, *Collected Works*, 3:29.

10. Dickson D. Bruce Jr., "National Identity and African-American Colonization, 1773–1817," *Historian* 58 (Autumn 1995): 15–28; Clegg, *Price of Liberty*, 22–25; William Lloyd Garrison, *Thoughts on African Colonization* (Boston: Garrison & Knapp, 1832), 5.

11. Leonard P. Richards, *"Gentlemen of Property and Standing": Anti-Abolition Mobs in Jacksonian America* (New York: Oxford University Press, 1970), 21–36; Charles N. Zucker, "The Free Negro Question: Race Relations in Antebellum Illinois, 1801–1860" (Ph.D. diss., Northwestern University, 1972), 191; Merton L. Dillon, "The Antislavery Movement in Illinois, 1809–1844" (Ph.D. diss., University of Michigan, 1951), 132–151; Paul M. Angle, *"Here I Have Lived": A History of Lincoln's Springfield, 1821–1865* (New Brunswick: Rutgers University Press, 1935), 52.

12. Basler, *Collected Works*, 2:131–132, 2:255–256, 2:298–299; 3:15; *Springfield Journal* in *Daily Missouri Republican* (St. Louis), February 7, 1858.

13. Basler, *Collected Works*, 2:132.

14. Ibid., 2:521. On civic and racial nationalisms, see Eric Foner, *Who Owns History?: Rethinking the Past in a Changing World* (New York: Hill & Wang, 2002), 151–157.

15. Philip S. Foner and George E. Walker, eds., *Proceedings of the Black State Conventions, 1840–1865*, 2 vols. (Philadelphia: Temple University Press, 1979), 2:60–64; Christopher R. Reed, *Black Chicago's First Century* (Columbia: University of Missouri Press, 2005), 1:106; Richard E. Hart, "Springfield's African-Americans as a Part of the Lincoln Community," *Journal of the Abraham Lincoln Association* 20 (Winter 1999): 48–53; *Chicago Press and Tribune*, August 16, 1868.

16. *New York Herald*, January 12, 1860.

17. Eric Foner, *Free Soil, Free Labor, Free Men: The Ideology of the Republican Party before the Civil War* (New York: Oxford University Press, 1970), 268–272; Francis P. Blair Jr., *The Destiny of the Races of This Continent* (Washington: Buell & Blanchard, 1859), 7–8; Francis P. Blair Jr. to Francis P. Blair, February 18, 1857, Blair Family Papers, Library of Congress; Joseph F. Newton, *Lincoln and Herndon* (Cedar Rapids: Torch Press, 1910), 114; Walter B. Stevens, "Lincoln and Missouri," *Missouri Historical Review* 10 (January 1916): 68; Basler, *Collected Works*, 2:298–299, 2:409–410, 3:233–34.

18. Foner and Walker, *Proceedings of the Black State Conventions*, 1:335; *Weekly Anglo-African*, May 19, 26, 1860, February 23, 1861; *Douglass' Monthly*, February 1859, 19; January 1861, 386; May 1861, 449.

19. Albert Mordell, ed., *Lincoln's Administration: Selected Essays by Gideon Welles* (New York: Twayne Publishers, 1960), 234; Howard K. Beale, ed., *Diary of Gideon Welles*, 3 vols. (New York: W. W. Norton, 1960), 1:150; Charles A. Barker, ed., *Memoirs of Elisha Oscar Crosby* (San Marino: Huntington Library, 1945), 87–90.

20. Ambrose W. Thompson to Lincoln, April 11, 1861, Thompson to Gideon Welles, August 8, 1861, Lincoln Papers; Basler, *Collected Works*, 4:547; Beale, *Diary of Gideon Welles*, 1:151.

21. Basler, *Collected Works*, 5:48; *New York Times*, December 4, 5, 6, 1861.

22. *Congressional Globe*, 37th Congress, 2d Session, 1605; James Mitchell, *Report on Colonization and Emigration* (Washington: Government Printing Office, 1862), 5; V. Jacque Voegeli, *Free but Not Equal: The Midwest and the Negro during the Civil War* (Chicago: University of Chicago Press, 1967), 25; *Official Opinions of the Attorneys General of the United States*, 12 vols. (Washington: Government Printing Office, 1852–70), 10:382–413.

23. Adams S. Hill to Sydney Howard Gay, August 25, 1862, Sydney Howard Gay Papers, Columbia University; Basler, *Collected Works*, 5:317–319.

24. Basler, *Collected Works*, 5:370–375.

25. Edward M. Thomas to Lincoln, August 16, 1862, Lincoln Papers; John Niven, ed., *The Salmon P. Chase Papers*, 5 vols. (Kent: Kent State University Press,

1993–98), 1:362; *Douglass's Monthly*, October 1862, 722–723; *Christian Recorder*, September 27, 1862; *New York Times*, October 3, 1862.

26. *National Anti-Slavery Standard*, August 20, 1862; Voegeli, *Free but Not Equal*, 34; *Chicago Tribune*, August 22, 1862.

27. Beale, *Diary of Gideon Welles*, 1:123, 1:152, 1:475–476; Niven, *Chase Papers*, 1:348–352, 1:393–402; Mordell, *Lincoln's Administration*, 105–107; Joseph Henry to Frederick W. Seward, September 5, 1862, unknown to Joseph Henry, September 5, 1862, Lincoln Papers; *Papers Relating to the Foreign Relations of the United States, 1861–1862* (Washington: Government Printing Office, 1862), 883–884, 889, 893, 904.

28. Basler, *Collected Works*, 5:520–521, 5:530–535.

29. Ibid., 6:41; Howard K. Beale, ed., *The Diary of Edward Bates, 1859–1866* (Washington: Government Printing Office, 1933), 268.

30. Basler, *Collected Works*, 6:28–30.

31. Allan G. Bogue, "William Parker Cutler's Congressional Diary of 1862–63, *Civil War History* 33 (December 1987): 328; Thomas S. Malcolm, Memorandum, February 4, 1863, J. P. Usher to William H. Seward, April 22, 1863, Usher to Edwin M. Stanton, April 28, 1863, Usher to John Hodge, May 11, 1863, Letters Sent, September 8, 1858–February 1, 1872; John Hodge to Usher, May 6, 14, 1863, Communications Relating to Colonization in British Honduras, Records of the Office of the Secretary of the Interior Relating to the Suppression of the African Slave Trade and Negro Colonization, 1854–1872, RG 48, National Archives; *New York Times*, May 18, 1863.

32. J. P. Usher to Lincoln, May 18, 1863, Letters Sent, September 8, 1858–February 1, 1872; James Mitchell to Lincoln, November 25, 1863 (copy), Communication Relating to Rev. James Mitchell, RG 48, National Archives; *Congressional Globe*, 38th Congress, 1st Session, Appendix, 46–47.

33. *Douglass' Monthly*, February 1863, 786; Floyd J. Miller, *Search for a Black Nationality: Black Emigration and Colonization, 1787–1863* (Urbana: University of Illinois Press, 1975), 261; Basler, *Collected Works*, 6:410; 8:272; Michael Vorenberg, "Slavery Reparations in Theory and Practice," in Brian Dirck, ed., *Lincoln Emancipated: The President and the Politics of Race* (DeKalb: Northern Illinois University Press, 2007), 125–127; Herman Belz, *A New Birth of Freedom: The Republican Party and Freedmen's Rights, 1861–1866* (Westport: Greenwood Press, 1976), 72; Michael Vorenberg, *Final Freedom: The Civil War, the Abolition of Slavery, and the Thirteenth Amendment* (New York: Cambridge University Press, 2001), 106.

34. J. P. Usher to Charles K. Tuckerman, April 17, July 8, 1863, April 5, 1864, Letters Sent, September 8, 1858–February 1, 1872, RG 48, National Archives; James De Long to Henry Conrad, June 25, 1863, Lincoln Papers; Basler, *Collected Works*, 7:164; J. P. Usher to Lincoln, May 18, 1863, Letters Sent, September 8, 1858–February 1,

1872, RG 48, National Archives; Michael Burlingame and John R. Ettinger, eds., *Inside Lincoln's White House: The Complete Civil War Diary of John Hay* (Carbondale: Southern Illinois University Press, 1997), 217.

35. Basler, *Collected Works*, 6:365; 7:185, 7:243; Beale, Diary of Gideon Welles, 2:237; Alexander H. Stephens, *A Constitutional View of the Late War between the States*, 2 vols. (Philadelphia: National Publishing Co., 1868–70), 2:613–614.

36. *Douglass' Monthly*, October 1862, 724–725.

37. Basler, *Collected Works*, 8, 403.

Legacies of Enslavement

Research for this essay derives from the AHRC (UK) and SSHRC (Canada) funded project: *Documenting Louisiana Sugar, 1845–1917* (2003–8), www.sussex.ac.uk/louisianasugar. Many thanks to Trevor Burnard, Robert Cook, Michael W. Fitzgerald, Rick Halpern, Moon-Ho Jung, Erik Mathisen, Susan E. O'Donovan, John C. Rodrigue, Jarod Roll, Adam Rothman, and Clive Webb for comments on this essay.

1. *The Iberville South* (Plaquemine), February 14, 1880; Elaine Frantz Parsons, "Midnight Rangers: Costume and Performance in the Reconstruction-Era Ku Klux Klan," *Journal of American History* 92 (December 2005): 811–836.

2. J. Carlyle Sitterson, *Sugar Country: The Cane Sugar Industry in the South, 1753–1950* (Lexington: University of Kentucky Press, 1953), 13–34; Alex Lichtenstein, "Rethinking Agrarian Labor in the US South," *Journal of Peasant Studies* 35 (October 2008): 621–635; Ira Berlin, *The Making of African America: The Four Great Migrations* (New York: Viking, 2010), 138–143.

3. John C. Rodrigue, *Reconstruction in the Cane Fields: From Slavery to Free Labor in Louisiana's Sugar Parishes, 1862–1880* (Baton Rouge: Louisiana State University Press, 2001); Rebecca J. Scott, *Degrees of Freedom: Louisiana and Cuba after Slavery* (Cambridge: Harvard University Press, 2005); Moon-Ho Jung, *Coolies and Cane: Race, Labor, and Sugar in the Age of Emancipation* (Baltimore: Johns Hopkins University Press, 2006).

4. Stephen Kantrowitz, *Ben Tillman and the Reconstruction of White Supremacy* (Chapel Hill: University of North Carolina Press, 2000), 5; George M. Fredrickson, *The Black Image in the White Mind: The Debate on Afro-American Character and Destiny, 1817–1914* (New York: Harper & Row, 1971), 180, 187; Edward Blum, *Reforging the White Republic: Race, Religion, and American Nationalism, 1865–1898* (Baton Rouge: Louisiana State University Press, 2005), 1–19; Mark Wahlgreen Summers, *A Dangerous Stir: Fear, Paranoia, and the Making of Reconstruction* (Chapel Hill: University of North Carolina Press, 2009), 245–272; Hannah Rosen, *Terror in the Heart*

of Freedom: Citizenship, Sexual Violence, and the Meaning of Race in the Postemancipation South (Chapel Hill: University of North Carolina Press, 2009), 6–16.

5. Thomas C. Holt, *The Problem of Freedom: Race, Labor, and Politics in Jamaica and Britain, 1832–1938* (Baltimore: Johns Hopkins University Press, 1992), 6. On the "labor problem," Matthew Pratt Guterl, *American Mediterranean: Southern Slaveholders in the Age of Emancipation* (Cambridge: Harvard University Press, 2008), 122–123; Amy Dru Stanley, *From Bondage to Contract: Wage Labor, Marriage, and the Market in the Age of Slave Emancipation* (Cambridge: Cambridge University Press, 1998), 77.

6. Thavolia Glymph, *Out of the House of Bondage: The Transformation of the Plantation Household* (Cambridge: Cambridge University Press, 2008), 134; Leon F. Litwack, *Been in the Storm So Long: The Aftermath of Slavery* (London: Athlone Press, 1979), 387–449; Frederick Cooper, "Back to Work: Categories, Boundaries, and Connections in the Study of Labour," in *Racializing Class, Classifying Race: Labour and Difference in Britain, the USA, and Africa*, ed. Peter Alexander and Rick Halpern (Basingstoke: Macmillan, 2000), 228.

7. Richard Follett, *The Sugar Masters: Planters and Slaves in Louisiana's Cane World, 1820–1860* (Baton Rouge: Louisiana State University, 2005), 14–45; Karl Joseph Menn, *The Large Slaveholders of Louisiana—1860* (New Orleans: Pelican, 1964), 6–31. One hogshead contained 1000–1200 lbs of sugar.

8. Timothy Flint, *The History and Geography of the Mississippi Valley*, 2 vols. (Cincinnati: E. H. Flint, 1832), 1:244–245; *Daily Picayune* (New Orleans), July 9, 1862; Thomas C. Holt, "Marking: Race, Race-Making, and the Writing of History," *American Historical Review* (February 1995): 7; Walter Johnson, *Soul by Soul: Life inside the Antebellum Slave Market* (Cambridge: Harvard University Press, 1999), 136–161.

9. Follett, *Sugar Masters*, 131–218.

10. Vol. 3, Journal of Magnolia Plantation, October 1859–January 1863, Henry Clay Warmoth Papers, Southern Historical Collection, The Wilson Library, University of North Carolina at Chapel Hill (UNC), see August 11, 1862, August 16, 1862, October 22, 1862, September 6, 1862, January 25, 1863.

11. "Memorandum of a Contract between the United States and Planters in Two Louisiana Parishes & General Order No. 91" and "General Order 23, Headquarters, Department of the Gulf, 3 February, 1864," in Ira Berlin, Thavolia Glymph, Joseph P. Reidy, Leslie S. Rowland, and Julie Saville, *Freedom: A Documentary History of Emancipation, 1861–1867. Series 1*, vol. 3, *The Wartime Genesis of Free Labor: The Lower South* (Cambridge: Cambridge University Press, 1990), 383–387; 512–517, 515; *New York Times*, February 11, 1863, quoted in William F. Messner, *Freedmen and the Ideology of Free Labor: Louisiana, 1862–1865* (Lafayette: University

of Southwestern Louisiana Press, 1978), 53; Paul D. Escott, *"What Shall We Do with the Negro?": Lincoln, White Racism, and Civil War America* (Charlottesville: University of Virginia Press, 2009), 100.

12. "Testimony of the Superintendent of Negro Labor," February 6, 1864, in Berlin et al., *Freedom: Series 1*, 3:520; John M. Sacher, *A Perfect War of Politics: Parties, Politicians, and Democracy in Louisiana, 1824–1861* (Baton Rouge: Louisiana State University Press, 2003), 181–189, 287–301; Escott, *What Shall We Do*, 106.

13. Thomas W. Knox, *Camp-Fire and Cotton-Field: Southern Adventure* (repr., Whitefish, MT: Kessinger Publishing, 2004), 205. On the state, Erik Thomas Mathisen, "Pledges of Allegiance: State Formation in Mississippi between Slavery and Redemption" (Ph.D. diss., University of Pennsylvania, 2009), 81–120.

14. *New Orleans Tribune*, December 8, 1864, June 10, 1865. Also see Ted Tunnell, *Crucible of Reconstruction: War, Radicalism, and Race in Louisiana* (Baton Rouge: Louisiana State University Press, 1976), 85; C. Peter Ripley, *Slaves and Freedmen in Civil War Louisiana* (Baton Rouge: Louisiana State University Press, 1976), 75.

15. Julia A. Johnson to anonymous, 10 November 1865, Weeks (David and Family) Papers, Louisiana and Lower Mississippi Valley Collections, Hill Memorial Library, Louisiana State University (LSU); J. H. Duganne, *Camps and Prisons: Twenty Months in the Department of the Gulf* (New York: J. B. Robens, 1865), 36. On freedpeoples' expectations, Steven Hahn, Steven F. Miller, Susan E. O'Donovan, John C. Rodrigue, and Leslie S. Rowland, *Freedom: A Documentary History of Emancipation, 1861–1867. Series 3*, vol. 1, *Land and Labor, 1865* (Chapel Hill: University of North Carolina Press, 2008), 1–85; Susan Eva O'Donovan, *Becoming Free in the Cotton South* (Cambridge: Harvard University Press, 2007); Steven Hahn, *The Political Worlds of Slavery and Freedom* (Cambridge: Harvard University Press, 2009), 55–114.

16. Vol. 36. Plantation Diary, 1863–68, 4 March 1863, 14 November 1863, Minor (William J. and Family) Papers, LSU; J. Carlyle Sitterson, "The Transition from Slave to Free Economy on the William J. Minor Plantations," *Agricultural History* 17 (October 1943): 216–224.

17. Vol. 36, January 3, 1863, February 26, 1863, March 4, 1863, September 26, 1863, October 7, 1863, November 5, 1863, see particularly November 14, 1863, November 27, 1863, Minor Papers, LSU.

18. Testimony of William J. Minor, 25 April 1865, Smith-Brady Commission, in Berlin et al, *Freedom: Series 1*, 3:600–602; Vol. 34, Plantation Diary 1861, "Rules and Regulations on Governing Southdown and Hollywood Plantations"; List of Cane Hands 1863–1864; Vol. 36, January 14, 1866, also September 4, 1865, September 23, 1865, January 10, 1866, Minor Papers, LSU. On labor companies, Paul K. Eiss, "A Share in the Land: Freedpeople and the Government of Labour in Southern Louisiana, 1862–1865," *Slavery and Abolition* 19 (April 1998): 46–89.

19. Edward King, *The Great South: A Record of Journeys*, ed. W. Magruder Drake and Robert R. Jones (repr., Baton Rouge: Louisiana State University Press, 1972), 32; *Iberville South*, December 28, 1867; unknown to Julia A. Johnson, August 5, 1865, Weeks Papers, LSU. On loss of mastery, see James L. Roark, *Masters without Slaves: Southern Planters in the Civil War and Reconstruction* (New York: W. W. Norton, 1977), 68–108; Bertram Wyatt-Brown, *The Shaping of Southern Culture: Honor, Grace, and War, 1760s–1880s* (Chapel Hill: University of North Carolina Press, 2001), 254–258, 281–293; Anne Sarah Rubin, *A Shattered Nation: The Rise and Fall of the Confederacy, 1861–1868* (Chapel Hill: University of North Carolina Press, 2005), 100–102, 211–213.

20. *The Pioneer of Assumption* (Napoleonville), July 28, 1877, October 16, 1880; John T. Trowbridge, *A Picture of the Desolated States and the Work of Restoration, 1865–1868* (Hartford: L. Stebbins, 1868), 392.

21. On black codes, Ordinance by the Board of Police, Opelousas, LA, July 15, 1865, in Hahn et al., *Freedom, Series 3*, 1:237–239; Dan T. Carter, *When the War Was Over: The Failure of Self-Reconstruction in the South, 1865–1867* (Baton Rouge: Louisiana State University Press, 1985), 187–191, 216–231; Harold D. Woodman, *New South–New Law: The Legal Foundations of Credit and Labor Relations in the Postbellum Agricultural South* (Baton Rouge: Louisiana State University Press, 1995), 8–13, 62–66.

22. Lawrence Powell, "Centralization and Its Discontents in Reconstruction Louisiana," *Studies in American Political Development* 20 (Fall 2006): 105–131; Charles Vincent, *Black Legislators in Louisiana during Reconstruction* (Baton Rouge: Louisiana State University Press, 1976), 71, 8; Henry Clay Warmoth, *War, Politics, and Reconstruction: Stormy Days in Louisiana* (Columbia: University of South Carolina Press, 2006), xx–xxiv, 79–84; Justin A. Nystrom, *New Orleans after the Civil War* (Baltimore: Johns Hopkins University Press, 2010), 82–114.

23. John Richard Dennett, *The South as It Is, 1865–1866*, ed. Henry M. Christman (New York: Viking Press, 1965), 318–329, quote on 318; Whitelaw Reid, *After the War: A Southern Tour, May 1, 1865 to May 1, 1866* (Cincinnati: Moore, Wilstach & Baldwin, 1866), 278.

24. Plantation Payrolls, 1868–1874, Benjamin Tureaud Family Papers, LSU; "Report of Work on Highland in January 1873," Labor Lists, Notes, Receipts 1873, Pugh Family Papers, Center for American History, University of Texas at Austin; List of Workers on Belair, April 30, 1868, Dymond Family Papers, Historic New Orleans Collection (HNOC); John C. Rodrigue, "The Freedmen's Bureau and Wage Labor in Louisiana's Sugar Region," in *The Freedmen's Bureau and Reconstruction: Reconsiderations*, ed. Paul A. Cimballa and Randall M. Miller (New York: Fordham University Press, 1999), 193–218.

25. *The Sugar Planter* (Port Allen), April 3, 1869; Vol. 2, Plantation Diary, April 19, 1867, December 31, 1867, Vol. 3, Plantation Diary, July 4, 1868, DeClouet (Alex-

andre E. and Family) Papers, LSU; "Letters of a Yankee Sugar Planter," *Journal of Southern History* 6 (1940): 553; *Iberville South*, June 22, 1867; Andrew H. Gay to Edward J. Gay, January 7, 1874, Gay (Edward and Family) Papers, LSU.

26. Samuel Cranwill to Edward J. Gay, January 18, 1873, Gay Papers, LSU; L. Bouchereau, *Statement of the Sugar and Rice Crops Made in Louisiana in 1869–70* (New Orleans: Young, Bright & Co., 1870), ix; W. P. Flowers to Thomas B. Pugh, January 8, 1874, Pugh (Colonel W. W. and Family) Papers, LSU; *Iberville South*, February 13, 1869. On calculations of relative wages, see William H. Harris, *Louisiana Products, Resources, and Attractions with a Sketch of the Parishes* (New Orleans: Times-Democrat, 1881), 57–58 (total wages of laborer on sugar plantation, $378.10; on cotton plantation, $265.60; of a common laborer in North, $144.30).

27. *The Planters' Banner* (Franklin), December 28, 1867; *Iberville South*, September 19, 1868; *St. James Sentinel* (Convent), May 22, 1875; Samuel Cranwill to Edward J. Gay, December 18, 1871, Gay Papers, LSU; John C. Rodrigue, "'The Great Law of Demand and Supply': The Contest over Wages in Louisiana's Sugar Region, 1870–1880," *Journal of Agricultural History* 72 (Spring 1998): 170–173.

28. *Iberville South*, November 2, 1867, February 17, 1866, March 10, 1866. On notions of black intransigence, see William Cohen, *At Freedom's Edge: Black Mobility and the Southern White Quest for Racial Control, 1861–1915* (Baton Rouge: Louisiana State University, 1991), 176; Demetrius L. Eudell, *The Political Languages of Emancipation in the British Caribbean and the U.S. South* (Chapel Hill: University of North Carolina Press, 2002), 52–58; Saidya V. Hartman, *Scenes of Subjection: Terror, Slavery, and Self-Making in Nineteenth Century America* (New York: Oxford University Press, 1997), 126–130.

29. Edward Bartlett Rugemer, *The Problem of Emancipation: The Caribbean Roots of the American Civil War* (Baton Rouge: Louisiana State University, 2008), 267, 268; David Brion Davis, *Challenging the Boundaries of Slavery* (Cambridge: Harvard University Press, 2003), 81–85; Eric Foner, *Nothing But Freedom: Emancipation and Its Legacy* (Baton Rouge: Louisiana State University Press, 1983), 42–44.

30. Duncan S. Cage to J. Madison Wells, 15 December 1865, in Hahn et al., *Freedom, Series 3*, 1:873; Fredrickson, *Black Image*, 188, 230; Wilma King, ed., *A Northern Woman in the Plantation South: Letters of Tryphena Blanche Holder Fox, 1856–1876* (Columbia: University of South Carolina Press, 1993), 228, 210.

31. John Michael Vlach, *Back of the Big House: The Architecture of Plantation Slavery* (Chapel Hill: University of North Carolina Press, 1993), 162; Follett, *Sugar Masters*, 179–182; Rebecca J. Scott, "Defining the Boundaries of Freedom in the World of Cane: Cuba, Brazil, and Louisiana after Emancipation," *American Historical Review* 99 (February 1994): 76; Anthony E. Kaye, *Joining Places: Slave Neighborhoods in the Old South* (Chapel Hill: University of North Carolina, 2007), 32–50.

32. On independent production, Vol. 46, Plantation Ledger, 1858–1872, "Wages Paid to Laborers, 1870," Benjamin Tureaud Family Papers, LSU; Vol. 13, Account Book, 1882–1883, Andrew McCollam Papers, UNC; Nancy D. Bercaw, *Gendered Freedoms: Race, Rights, and the Politics of the Delta, 1861–1875* (Gainesville: University Press of Florida, 2003), 122; Sharon Ann Holt, *Making Freedom Pay: North Carolina Freedpeople Working for Themselves, 1865–1900* (Athens: University of Georgia Press, 2000), 2. On silence, Mark M. Smith, *Listening to Nineteenth-Century America* (Chapel Hill: University of North Carolina Press, 2001), 19–22.

33. *Planters' Banner*, September 8, 1869, August 28, 1868, December 28, 1867. On insurrection fears, see Hahn et al., *Freedom, Series 3*, 1:796–808, 900.

34. *Planters' Banner*, August 28, 1868; Vol. 3, Plantation Diary, September 20, 1868; Vol. 4, Plantation Diary, October 15, 1868, DeClouet Papers, LSU; Stephen Kantrowitz, "One Man's Mob Is Another Man's Militia: Violence, Manhood, and Authority in Reconstruction South Carolina," in *Jumpin' Jim Crow: Southern Politics from Civil War to Civil Rights*, ed. Jane Dailey, Glenda Gilmore, and Bryant Simon (Princeton: Princeton University Press, 2000), 69–71.

35. *Sugar Planter*, February 10, 1866; Daniel Dennett, *Louisiana as It Is* (New Orleans: Eureka Press, 1876), 169. On enthusiasm for small-holding cane farmers, see Charles Nordhoff, *The Cotton States in the Spring and Summer of 1875* (New York: D. Appleton, 1876), 71; *De Bow's Review*, 5 (April 1868): 421.

36. *Planters' Banner*, December 7, 1870; *Thibodaux Sentinel*, February 17, 1872, August 12, 1865, January 25, 1873; *Louisiana Sugar Bowl* (New Iberia), June 19, 1873; *Sugar Planter*, January 16, 1869. On Helper, see David Brown, *Southern Outcast: Hinton Rowan Helper and the Impending Crisis of the South* (Baton Rouge: Louisiana State University Press, 2006), 91–123; Jung, *Coolies*, 163.

37. William H. Harris, *Louisiana Products, Resources, and Attractions with a Sketch of the Parishes* (New Orleans: Times-Democrat, 1881), 9.

38. *Attakapas Register* (Morgan City), March 31, 1877; *Pioneer of Assumption*, August 18, 1877; *Louisiana Sugar Bowl*, December 24, 1874. On black tenancy, see Sean Kelly, "A Texas Peasantry? Black Smallholders in the Texas Sugar Bowl, 1865–1890," *Slavery and Abolition* 28 (August 2007): 193–209.

39. *Planters' Banner*, November 9, 1870, November 23, 1870; *Iberville South*, February 23, 1867; L. Bouchereau, *Statement of the Sugar and Rice Crops Made in Louisiana in 1868–69* (New Orleans: Young, Bright & Co., 1869), viii.

40. Bouchereau, *Statement 1868–69*, viii; *Planters' Banner*, November 23, 1870; L. Bouchereau, *Statement of the Sugar and Rice Crops Made in Louisiana in 1870–71* (New Orleans: Young, Bright & Co., 1872), xix; Richard J. Amundson, "Oakley Plantation: A Post Civil War Venture in Louisiana Sugar," *Louisiana History* 9 (1968): 27–28; *Iberville South*, January 15, 1881, March 12, 1881; additionally see *Thibodaux Sentinel*, May 11, 1872; Report of the Bureau of Immigration to the General Assem-

bly of Louisiana (New Orleans: A. L. Lee, 1869), 29; Vol. 4, Journal 1870–1872, April 13, 1871, May 20, 1871, September 4, 1871, February 25, 1872, Pugh-Williams-Mayes Family Papers, LSU; Nancy C. Dymond to John Dymond, September 26, 1881, Dymond Family Papers, HNOC; Danish Emigrant Agency to Edward J. Gay, December 14, 1869, Labor Contract October 16, 1871, Gay Papers, LSU; *Planters' Banner*, September 15, 1869, September 21, 1870, November 9, 1870, December 7, 1870, February 1, 1870, March 8, 1871; Richard Follett and Rick Halpern, "From Slavery to Freedom in Louisiana's Sugar Country: Changing Labor Systems and Workers' Power," in *Sugar, Slavery, and Society: Perspectives on the Caribbean, India, the Mascarenes, and the United States*, ed. Bernard Moitt (Gainesville: University of Florida Press, 2004), 135–156.

41. *Louisiana Sugar Bowl*, April 27, 1871, July 6, 1871; *Sugar Planter*, June 12, 1869; *Iberville South*, April 13, 1867; *Donaldsonville Chief*, January 17, 1874; Jung, *Coolies*, 96–97.

42. *Planters' Banner*, July 21, 1869; *Louisiana Sugar Bowl*, August 31, 1871, April 27, 1871, July 15, 1880, March 2, 1882, also October 12, 1871; *Planters' Banner*, February 9, 1870, also August 11, 1869, January 19, 1870, April 13, 1870, September 21, 1870, November 9, 1870; *Le Louisianais* (Convent), October 23, 1869; *Harpers Weekly*, September 11, 1869.

43. On the Virginia trade, see *Planters' Banner*, January 19, 1870; Robert C. Martin to Maggie Martin, August 30, 1870, Martin-Pugh Papers, Ellender Memorial Library, Nicholls State University, Thibodaux (NSU); *Sugar Planter*, October 23, 1869; Andrew H. Gay to Edward J. Gay, August 13, 1870, and Roman Daigre to Edward J. Gay, December 26, 1871, Gay Papers LSU.

44. *Iberville South*, February 23, 1867.

45. *Iberville South*, September 19, 1868; Hepworth, *Whip, Hoe, Sword*, 98; Robert C. Martin to Robert C. Martin Jr., November 9, 1875, Martin-Pugh Papers, NSU; Vol 1, Plantation Diary, October 18, 1866, DeClouet Papers, LSU; Vol. 21, January 12, 1887, Vol. 22, January 30/31, 1888, William Porcher Miles Volumes, UNC.

46. *New Iberia Enterprise*, March 21, 1885; Trowbridge, *Desolated States*, 389; *St. James Sentinel*, May 22, 1875; Rodrigue, *Reconstruction*, 111–112. On northern masters, see Lawrence N. Powell, *New Masters: Northern Planters during the Civil War and Reconstruction* (New Haven: Yale University Press, 1980), 76, 103–122. On planter relocation, see Guterl, *American Mediterranean*, 79–113; Roark, *Masters without Slaves*, 120–131.

47. Edward J. Gay to Samuel Cricklow, October 7, 1874, Gay Papers, LSU; Thomas Affleck, *The Sugar Plantation Record and Account Book No. 2* (New Orleans: B. M. Norman, 1854); Samuel Cranwill to Edward J. Gay, October 8, 1874, Edward J. Gay to Samuel Hollingsworth, October 31, 1874, Samuel Cranwill to Edward J. Gay, May 13, 1873, Gay Papers, LSU. On despair among planters, see Annie to Thomas B.

Pugh, November 23, 1876, Pugh (Colonel W.W. and Family) Papers, LSU; *Louisiana Sugar Bowl*, June 19, 1873. On the need for managerial rigor, see Vol. 4, Donelson Caffery Letter Book, Bethia R. Caffery to Donelson Caffery, August 20, 1877, Caffery (Donelson and Family) Papers, LSU. Additionally, Joseph P. Reidy, "Mules and Machines and Men: Field Labor on Louisiana Sugar Plantations, 1887-1915," *Agricultural History* 72 (Spring 1998): 191.

48. *Louisiana Sugar Bowl*, January 15 and January 22, 1874; Rodrigue, *Reconstruction*, 161-165; Scott, *Degrees*, 55-56; John Heitmann, *The Modernization of the Louisiana Sugar Industry, 1830-1910* (Baton Rouge: Louisiana State University Press, 1987), 50-59.

49. *Louisiana Democrat*, May 13, 1873, quoted in LeeAnna Keith, *The Colfax Massacre: The Untold Story of Black Power, White Terror, and the Death of Reconstruction* (New York: Oxford University Press, 2008), 108; "Address to White Citizens of St Martins Parish," June 14, 1874, DeClouet Papers, LSU; Michael W. Fitzgerald, *Splendid Failure: Postwar Reconstruction in the American South* (Chicago: Ivan R. Dee, 2007), 92.

50. Louis Alfred Wiltz, *The Great Mississippi Flood of 1874: Its Extent, Duration and Effects* (New Orleans: Picayune Steam Book, 1874), 4; Christopher Morris, *The Big Muddy: An Environmental History of the Mississippi and Its Peoples from Hernando de Soto to Hurricane Katrina* (New York: Oxford University Press, 2012); James K. Hogue, *Uncivil War: Five New Orleans Street Battles and the Rise and Fall of Radical Reconstruction* (Baton Rouge: Louisiana State University Press, 2006), 116-143; Nystrom, *New Orleans*, 160-185; Marek D. Steedman, "Rhetoric, Rebirth, and Redemption: The Rhetoric of White Supremacy in Post-Civil War Louisiana," *Historical Reflections* 35 (Spring 2009): 97-113.

51. Eric Foner, *Reconstruction: America's Unfinished Revolution, 1863-1877* (New York: Harper Row, 1988), 582, 529-531; Joe Gray Taylor, *Louisiana Reconstructed, 1863-1877* (Baton Rouge: Louisiana State University Press, 1974), 481-505.

52. *Donaldsonville Chief*, October 20, 1877. On the LSPA, see Heitmann, *Modernization*, 68-97; Sitterson, *Sugar Country*, 252-255; Vol. 1, Minutes, 1877-1891, Louisiana Sugar Planters Association Papers, LSU (see, e.g., entries for November 20, 1877, January 3, 1878, January 28, 1878, February 12, 1880); *The Pioneer of Assumption*, December 15, 1877, January 12, 1878, February 16, 1878.

53. *Iberville South*, July 4, 1885; Hogue, *Uncivil War*, 187-194.

54. Rodrigue, *Reconstruction*, 180. On "Kansas Fever" and strike action, see Vol. 6, Plantation Diary, June 25, 1879, William A. Shaffer Papers, UNC; *Louisiana Sugar Bowl*, October 9, 1879, July 15, 1880; Rick Halpern, "Solving the 'Labour Problem': Race, Work, and the State in the Sugar Industries of Louisiana and Natal, 1870-1910," *Journal of Southern African Studies* 30 (March 2004): 21-22.

55. Mary Pugh to Edward F. Pugh, November 25, 1887, Mary W. Pugh Papers, LSU; Rebecca J. Scott, "Fault Lines, Color Lines, and Party Lines: Race, Labor, and Collective Action in Louisiana and Cuba, 1862–1912," in *Beyond Slavery: Explorations of Race, Labor, and Citizenship in Postemancipation Societies*, ed. Frederick Cooper, Thomas C. Holt, and Rebecca J. Scott (Chapel Hill: University of North Carolina Press, 2000), 80–82.

Conclusion

1. Frederick Douglass, "Speech at the Civil Rights Mass Meeting," Lincoln Hall, Washington, D.C., October 22, 1883; http://memory.loc.gov, accessed March 28, 2009; Frederick Douglass, *Life and Times of Frederick Douglass* (New York: Collier Books, 1962), 539.

2. Michele Mitchell, *Righteous Propagation: African Americans and the Politics of Racial Destiny after Reconstruction* (Chapel Hill: University of North Carolina Press, 2004), 5; Steven Hahn, *A Nation under Our Feet: Black Political Struggles in the Rural South from Slavery to the Great Migration* (Cambridge: Harvard University Press, 2003), 319–320; "Testimony of Henry Adams regarding the Negro Exodus," in Herbert Aptheker, ed., *A Documentary History of the Negro People in the United States* (New York: Citadel Press, 1951), 715; Heather Cox Richardson, *The Death of Reconstruction: Race, Labor, and Politics in the Post–Civil War North, 1865–1901* (Cambridge: Harvard University Press, 2001), 156–182; Nell Irvin Painter, *Exodusters: Black Migration to Kansas after Reconstruction* (New York: Alfred A. Knopf, 1977), 71–107.

3. David W. Blight, *Frederick Douglass' Civil War: Keeping Faith in Jubilee* (Baton Rouge: Louisiana State University Press, 1989), 217; "Testimony of Henry Adams"; John Dittmer, "The Education of Henry McNeal Turner," in *Black Leaders of the Nineteenth Century*, ed. Leon Litwack and August Meier (Urbana: University of Illinois Press, 1988), 271; Leslie A. Schwalm, *Emancipation's Diaspora: Race and Reconstruction in the Upper Midwest* (Chapel Hill: University of North Carolina Press, 2009), 191.

GUIDE TO FURTHER READING

❧

The African American struggle to define real, practical, and meaningful freedom in the age of emancipation (and beyond) remains one of the most arresting episodes in American history. Hundreds of books and articles attest to the enduring fascination students and scholars alike find with slavery and emancipation. The notes and text of this book refer to many of the key published works, but for student and general readers seeking a brief guide to the most significant works on slavery, emancipation, and post-emancipation America, we include an introductory guide to the historiography.

Black racial inferiority characterized the earliest scholarly works on African American history. Ulrich B. Phillips's *American Negro Slavery* (1918) treated black Americans as beneficiaries of slavery, while turn-of-the-century racism similarly marred William Archibald Dunning's (1907) scholarship on Reconstruction, particularly in his approach toward former slaves, whom Dunning considered unfit for self-governance. Although W. E. B. Du Bois's *Black Reconstruction in America* (1935) demonstrated how black people shaped the bi-racial politics of the late 1860s, the tendency within interwar scholarship was to treat the slaves and freedpeople as objects (both victims and beneficiaries) rather than as agents demonstrating the remotest of free will.

Kenneth Stampp's *The Peculiar Institution* (1956) began the historiographical revision. It promised a "completely objective study" of slavery without any preestablished assumptions of racial inferiority. Energized by the civil rights, student, black power, and feminist movements of the 1960s, scholars during the 1970s and 1980s fundamentally challenged the older interpretations, most particularly Stanley Elkins's *Slavery: A Problem in American Institutional and Intellectual Life* (1959). Drawing parallels with the Nazi death camps, Elkins argued that the closed and absolute power structures of American slavery prompted infantilization and the erasure of African culture among the enslaved. By contrast, in a series of pioneering texts, historians John Blassingame (*The Slave Community*, 1972), Charles Joyner (*Down by the Riverside*, 1984), Lawrence Levine (*Black Culture and Black Consciousness*, 1977), Sterling Stuckey (*Slave Culture*, 1987) and—as Walter Johnson details in this book—Herbert Gutman (*The Black Family in Slavery and Freedom*, 1976) emphasized the slaves' capacity to nurture a rich, durable, and protective cultural space for themselves. Within the antebellum slave community, enslaved peoples found solace in one another, in an Afro-creolized culture, and they conspired to undermine planter authority by acts of day-to-day resistance. Although the semi-autonomous community flourished best during the twilight hours, or *From Sundown to Sunup*, as George Rawick's 1972 landmark text observed, historians portrayed the culturally vibrant slave community as a nexus of black agency and empowerment.

Some scholars, notably Robert Fogel and Stanley Engerman in *Time on the Cross* (1974), challenged the separatist agent-centered interpretation, even suggesting that bondspeople absorbed the Protestant work ethic from their masters. The withering critique of *Time on the Cross* (led by Herbert Gutman, among others) ultimately underscored the coercive nature of American slavery. Slaves worked hard, to be sure, but this did not imply that they surrendered their own values for those of the masters. Eugene Genovese's *Roll, Jordan, Roll* (1972) accepted these core arguments. In his densely interpretive work, Genovese utilized the concepts of hegemony and paternalism to depict the slaveholders, while describing the process of accommodation and resistance on the part of the slaves. Genovese emphasized the imprint of these values and processes on the culture, religion, and modes of resistance exercised by the enslaved. Ever astute to the parameters of class and racial power within slavery, Genovese nevertheless detailed "the world the slaves made," a community of enslaved actors who attached independent religious and cultural meanings to their lives.

Although the scholarly revisionism of the 1970s and 1980s prompted some of the finest scholarship and fiercest debates, by the end of the decade, most historians portrayed a powerful, culturally rich, and relatively autonomous antebellum slave community. More recent scholarship has built upon the bedrock of agent-centered interpretations but has carefully shied from romanticizing the enslaved or underestimating slaveholders' power and authority. As Stephanie Camp observes in *Closer to Freedom* (2004), "Scholars of slavery now consciously explore the contradictory and paradoxical qualities in bondspeople's lives: for instance, the ways in which they were both agents and subjects, persons and property, and people who resisted and accommodated—sometimes in one and the same act" (p. 1). Key works in the past decade by Ira Berlin (*Generations of Captivity*, 2003), Steven Hahn (*A Nation under Our Feet*, 2003), and Anthony Kaye (*Joining Places*, 2007) have added considerably to our understanding of the spatial, temporal, and gender developments within American slavery, and they have traced the subtleties of resistance, community formation, and the proto-political consciousness of the enslaved. Other authors, including William Dusinberre (*Them Dark Days*, 1996), Richard Follett (*The Sugar Masters*, 2005), Walter Johnson (*Soul by Soul*, 1999), and Peter Kolchin (*Unfree Labor*, 1987), assess the influence and subtlety of slaveholder power and consider its impact on the scale and scope of slave resistance. No single book addresses the divergent themes and arguments within contemporary slave studies, but students will find Mark Smith's *Debating Slavery* (1998) and Peter Kolchin's *American Slavery* (rev. ed. 2003) particularly helpful.

Much like the history of slavery, the study of emancipation underwent revision in the wake of the civil rights movement. Writing *The Era of Reconstruction, 1865–1877* (1965), Kenneth Stampp set the agenda for subsequent scholarship. First, he attempted to overturn older and racist interpretations on black rule during Reconstruction and, second, he and fellow revisionists John Hope Franklin (*From Slavery to Freedom*, 1947) and Leon Litwack (*Been in the Storm So Long*, 1979) assessed how former slaves perceived and experienced freedom (as independent actors themselves). It was, however, Eric Foner who provided the definitive study of emancipation era America in *Reconstruction: America's Unfinished Revolution* (1988). By paying close attention to class, race, and the role played by African Americans in the social, political, and labor readjustments of Reconstruction, Foner examined why contract freedom proved especially challenging for landless former slaves who were forced to compete in Reconstruction-era labor markets. Foner nevertheless recognized that the expansion of voting rights and office holding among former slaves had enduring consequences. Rebuilding their families, churches, and communities, former slaves utilized their power at the ballot box to advance an agenda of racial and social progress until white conservatives regained political power.

Most modern scholarship on black life after slavery builds upon the key insights advanced by Foner and, although historians differ over the degree to which unity and collectivism trumped conflict and individualism within the black community, African American self-determination and agency remains axiomatic, if embattled. Particularly significant within this rich vein are studies by Thavolia Glymph (*Out of the House of Bondage*, 2008), Susan E. O'Donovan (*Becoming Free in the Cotton South*, 2007), John Rodrigue (*Reconstruction in the Cane Fields*, 2001), Julie Saville (*The Work of Reconstruction*, 1994), and Rebecca Scott (*Degrees of Freedom*, 2005). All students, however, should consult Steven Hahn's *A Nation under Our Feet* (2003); it is the most important book published on Reconstruction since Foner's 1988 study and among the most significant works published on nineteenth-century American history. Hahn extends the concept of black historical agency, contending that African Americans forged a collective identity in slavery, which developed during the political mobilization of Reconstruction, before emerging with the black nationalism of Garvey's UNIA. Rooted to the political, labor, and community struggles of the Reconstruction years, Hahn looks back to the origins of black mobilization in the slave quarters and forward to the mutual aid societies of the Great Migration. In so doing, Hahn's *Nation* links black history across time and space and, like Foner's *Reconstruction*, it promises to shape the direction of scholarly inquiry for a generation more. For students seeking detailed information on the political history of Reconstruction, see Michael Perman's influential monographs (*Reunion without Compromise*, 1973; *The Road to Redemption*, 1984) and, for an excellent overview, see Michael Fitzgerald's *Splendid Failure* (2007). On the historiography of Reconstruction, see Thomas J. Brown, ed., *Reconstructions* (2006); for those seeking documentary sources and among the best essays on the early years of Reconstruction, see the numerous edited volumes of *Freedom: A Documentary History of Emancipation* (1982–), edited by Ira Berlin, Leslie Rowland, and Steven Hahn.

Foner and Hahn's imprint on the history of emancipation continues apace. In his *The Political Worlds of Slavery and Freedom* (2009), Steven Hahn continues to track the evolution of black politics and the language and process of emancipation from the 1840s to the 1920s. Indeed, he suggests that flight during the Civil War may well have been "the greatest slave rebellion in modern history." Discussion of the role slaves played in the collapse of slavery is not new—Barbara Fields, among others, explored this in her influential study (*Slavery and Freedom on the Middle Ground*, 1985), but Hahn places wartime emancipation within a larger history of freedom. The degree to which former slaves shaped their freedom or were confined by economic and material factors is a question Richard Follett turns to in this volume and one that continues to animate much scholarship. The role Abraham Lincoln played in the emancipative process commands considerable scholarly attention. Foremost recent works on the racial politics of the president include Paul Escott's *"What Shall We Do with the Negro?"* (2009) and Eric Foner's *The Fiery Trial* (2010).

This short book engages with many of the central questions on slavery and emancipation. It does not do so exhaustively, but the issues of African American agency, self-determination, racial power, and authority animate this study, as does the enduring problem of defining freedom in the age of emancipation.

INDEX